BREAKING
the CHAINS

By the Supernatural Power of Jesus

S H A N N O N   B A U M

ISBN 979-8-88540-528-7 (paperback)
ISBN 979-8-88540-529-4 (digital)

Christian Faith Publishing
832 Park Avenue
Meadville, PA 16335
www.christianfaithpublishing.com

Printed in the United States of America

This book is dedicated to my Lord and Savior Jesus Christ. I wrote this for his glory and not my own. For those that are struggling with drugs and/or alcohol and for the ones who have loved ones lost in the life of addiction. There is hope; we serve an all-knowing omniscient God. He loves us and is waiting for us to call on him for help. Mathew 18:12 says he will leave the ninety-nine to go get that one that is lost. We need just to take that step of faith and know that without him, we cannot overcome the darkness that has us in bondage.

As someone that has come from that life of drugs and alcohol, I have firsthand experience on what a drug user and alcoholic feels and goes through. I know that deep dark pit of hopelessness, the feeling like this is who you are, and this is the way it will always be. We see ourselves stuck in a life of despair and hardship. We long to be like others that are clean and living a good life, but nope, that's not us, for we are cursed to live this life as our thoughts trap us in our addiction. The life of struggle from day to day, hustling for those drugs, feeling like they help the pain. No one understands the pain physically and emotionally. It is real, and drugs and or alcohol is what takes it away. The feeling is without these drugs, we couldn't survive or don't want to because without them, we cannot function. This life or should I say death is the only way we know how to carry on, to live. We are those outcasts, those losers. We are so hard on ourselves that we often ask God just to take us, and our life becomes meaningless. We have nothing to offer others, but pain and destruction and we know this. So we run away from all those we love and keep them at a distance, lying to them and keeping ourselves masked and in darkness for that is all we know. We believe the lies that the devil has engulfed us with. We will never be able to change; no one can help us. This is our destiny to live this way in pain and suffering, and only the drug is able to help us, or at least we convince ourselves of this and others. We eventually become masters of our own lies and deception.

It took me a lifetime or at least it felt like one to finally understand that I could not fight this battle of drug and alcohol use on my own and to realize that the way of the world is just a means to destroy us. We carry such enormous weight on our shoulders of worry, pain, and suffering. I can honestly say that I hated myself during my addiction. I was my worst critic, and I had so much bitterness and hate against so many. This sickness of drugs and alcohol, this demonic influence, kept me in darkness and constant suffering for many years of my life. There were times I just wanted to give up and die. I thank God that he allowed me to live through this.

Many of us go through trauma in our lives, and we use this trauma as an excuse to use. For so many years, that trauma kept me in bondage; it opened up a foothold for Satan to use me against others and myself. This is what the enemy does to destroy us. This is his tactic, because we come with brokenness; he uses that against us, because we don't know Jesus, we turn to drugs and alcohol, sexual immorality, and other sin to fill the hole of emptiness of that pain that lives in our life. For that moment, we become engulfed in that sin, feeling that euphoria that we've been chasing. Why, because it is a strategy of war from the enemy Satan to turn you against God and his people. You keep needing more and more of that sin every time to feel better until you're a puppet engulfed in complete sin and deception. Satan and his demons now have you doing their bidding (lying, stealing, killing). If you have been or are in this lifestyle, then you know exactly what I speak is true; you've seen demonic things you can't explain, and you have been there yourself, either possessed by that demon or mingling with the demonic.

When we experience blackouts from drunkenness, what do you think that is? That is the demon taking over us. Trying to shame us, lying to us so that we can hurt others or ourselves; sometimes, they succeed on their mission to destroy us. We don't remember this, of course, because they have taken over us because of our sin, we allow them to enter us by us going our own way. The world's way of sin, instead of God's way. We put ourselves in a vulnerable state where the enemy can attack us and overpower us, taking us as captives to do his bidding. You see, God is our father in heaven. He wants us to live under his protection under his household, but the only way we can do this is by following his rules, accepting Jesus as our savior, and turning from our sinful ways.

When we follow our Father's rules, we begin to mimic him, and he guides us in his righteousness. God is Love; he cannot dwell within hate just like light cannot dwell in darkness. Therefore, if we are in our sin, he cannot dwell within us, for it is sin and it is not of the Father. Therefore, Jesus came and sacrificed himself because only through his blood could humanity be saved; his blood is enough. Without Jesus, our sins could not be forgiven; therefore, we could not have God reside within us. When we ask for forgiveness through our Lord and Savior Jesus and do it wholeheartedly, our sins are washed away, making us clean and righteous, so God may live in us. Therefore, we must turn from our sin, continuing to sin in the same manner is not being wholehearted. You must give up the sin completely.

Trust in the Lord to give you strength to overcome temptation. God tells us in 2 Timothy 1:7, "For God did not give you a spirit of timidity, but a spirit of power, love and self-discipline." When we ask God to forgive us for using drugs, which is pharmacia (sorcery), we cannot go back to using and think that he will continue to forgive us if we deliberately know it is a sin and deliberately do it, then we go against God for our selfish needs; we feed our sinful flesh. The only way for forgiveness of that sin is asking Christ for forgiveness and turning away from it completely and wholeheartedly. Yes, we do fall short and sin; we are only human, but this is why Jesus suffered for us on that cross so we may come to him and be forgiven.

I have been addicted most of my life since I was twelve years old. It started with alcohol and weed, then went on to acid, cocaine, mushrooms, meth—pretty much did everything. I would get in trouble and stop for a while but then fall right back into using and usually worse off. It started out as having fun, but then I would use it to cover up my pain, trauma that I had suffered in my childhood, trying to erase the hurtful moments through drugs and alcohol. I overdosed on alcohol at fifteen because of my boyfriend that was cheating on me, and it wasn't that I was trying to kill myself, I just didn't want to feel the pain. Even when God saved me from death, which didn't stop me. I continued on the path of destruction; it led up to financial brokenness and losing of my jobs, the loss of all my material gains, and eventually loss of my freedom.

In 2009, I was heading home from work. I stopped at the gas station to pick up alcohol. I already had been drinking, but it wasn't enough—it never was. I had been in a fight with my boyfriend and didn't want to go home. I decided to go to the car wash during this time and wait for some friends to pick me up. I was intoxicated, and I'm sure others there around me could tell. As I'm drying my car in the wash stall, a cop pulls up behind me. She comes over and asks me if I could move my car so she could wash her unit. I agreed, got in my car, and pulled off to the side by the vacuums. As I got out to continue drying my car, the officer walked over to me and asked me what was wrong; she told me that my eyes were very red. She said that I looked intoxicated and proceeded to do a field sobriety check on me.

After completing the sobriety check, she then stated to me that she was placing me under arrest for DWI. I tried to get in my car and go. I didn't get far; in fact, I didn't get anywhere. She jumped in my window, grabbing my keys, and before I knew it, we ended up on the floor rolling around. Somehow, I ended up on top of her, as I heard sirens and saw cop cars rushing all around me. I was surrounded by other units and cops with guns drawn. I was told to get on my knees and put my hands behind my head. I was already on my knees, with my hands behind my head. An officer approached me and put handcuffs on me, and he pushed my face to the ground where he dislodged my front tooth. They picked me up from the handcuffs, which made me scream in pain from the tearing I could feel in my arm.

Then as I got up, I was Maced. I just don't mean one spray or two; it was more like emptying their cans on me with at least three cops spraying me. My hair was soaking wet, as I was bent over, letting my hair drip down. By now, I was yelling in pain and blind due to the Mace; my lungs were filled with what felt like pepper when you inhale it, I couldn't stop coughing, I was put in the back of the unit and was rubbing my eyes on the back of the seat, trying to get the Mace out and at the same time I was spitting out the Mace in the car because it was in my mouth choking me. I started to spit up the Mace, and the cop proceeded to put a gag bag over my head.

At that point, I thought I was going to die. I was slowly suffocating. I was driven to the police station where they led me to a worse off. My thoughts would tell me I would never feel good again physically or emotionally and the only thing that would help is the drugs. I lied to everyone around me, including myself, about how bad my addiction was. The drugs instantly made me feel better, and I just kept telling myself that this pain was real. I needed the drugs; after all, it was a prescription from the doctor.

You see, I never recovered from the pain of that surgery or the fall. Instead, the pain became worse over the years, and now it was not only in my shoulder but also in my back and legs. I began to manifest pain that was real because of my addiction and my lifestyle of sin. I was seeing a specialist and going through an MRI, being told I need back surgery and that my MRI showed that I had slipped discs and protruding discs, pinched nerve, sciatica—oh, not to mention I was also told I had a rare condition from genetics. A nerve casing that was too small causing the pinching of the nerves would require surgery. This is the information I was being fed by doctors because my pain was so bad or so I claimed. I had myself and everyone around me fooled about how much pain I was in.

I even convinced myself and the doctors that without the drugs, I couldn't walk without assistance with a walker or cane. Once I took those pills, the pain was gone for a moment. It would always come back worse and the higher my dose would have to be. So my pain pill addiction ramped up to a three hundred dollar a day habit. By now, I was going through my prescription within a week and then buying off the street and doing what I needed to get that drug (stealing). I was in so much pain or at least that's what the enemy had me convinced of, not only physical but also emotional. Little did I know this was all a tactic of the enemy.

You see, the physical pain was real. I could feel the pain, and the doctors also agreed that I had pain. The problem was that I was thirty-eight years old and crippled—why, because of an accident that my body easily could have healed from, but because of my addiction, I couldn't get that healing. The drugs would not allow my body to heal. I didn't want to be in pain, and I liked the high of the drugs and how they made me feel. A part of me knew that these drugs were keeping me sick, but I couldn't break free from them because the bondage was too strong. I would feel like I was going to die when I tried to get clean on my own. I felt great when I was high. I could clean and work and do things to make me feel normal. So I manipulated the doctors. I would limp a little more or go in with a walker instead of a cane or tell them how bad the pain was that I couldn't sleep. All these were manipulations to get more pills. My need for the drug was a hunger never satisfied.

My addiction was hopelessness. This is who I was going to be, I had accepted it. I couldn't go anywhere. My drugs made me a prisoner. Stuck in a situation that only led to my death, my children watched me destroy myself and they couldn't understand why Mom couldn't go with them anywhere to the zoo to the amusement park. I was in bondage to these drugs and the demons were not going to let me go. I could only think of getting high twenty-four hours a day, seven days a week. I was living in hell on earth, but I knew there was a God. I didn't know that I could be healed again, and God would forgive me. I had failed so many times that I didn't think I was worthy of saving. I thought because of my past sins, there was no way that God would heal me.

I believed that this was the way my life, this is who I was going to be. I had accepted the lie from Satan. I was hurting myself and everyone around me. I just couldn't stop. Along this destructive journey, I incurred more DWIs and went to jail at least three more times, but I kept telling myself that I needed these drugs and that I couldn't live without them. During the month of November 2017, I was in my car getting high; it was something I did. I would leave for the whole night where I could be alone and get high, and this was one of those times. I felt different though; it was a sadness and a sickness within that made me just break down and weep. I knew I was going to die; I could feel it. My outrageous need or hunger for drugs was out of control, and something deep down inside of me knew I was not going to last very much longer. It was at this point that I cried out to God and asked him for help. Because I knew I couldn't do this on my own and he would be the only one that could save me. That night, I sat in my car and just prayed and cried out for help. I surrendered my life to him.

Saved by His Grace and Mercy

December 16, 2017

I had been using and drinking that morning since around 7 a.m. Around 12, I broke my front tooth while forcing myself to eat something. I called the dentist, and they were able to take me that afternoon. I thought I could drive because I drove thousands of times high and drunk. When I got to the dentist, they knew I was drinking; they were only in my mouth. The girls in the front told me when they finished with my tooth that they called my husband (boyfriend). I asked them why. I got very angry as I walked out the door. I heard them say we called the cops as I was walking out. This really put me into fight or flight mode. I took off like a bat out of hell from there the cops caught up to me eventually and the chase began. I led the cops on a high-speed chase for about twenty miles. During that time, I hit two cars and a motorcycle. I woke up in hospital with my arm handcuffed to the rail on the bed and an officer standing over me looked at me and spoke, "Oh, so you woke up, well, you're the lucky one because the young boy you hit on the motorcycle is fighting for his life and probably won't make it through the night."

At that moment, confusion hit. I didn't remember what happened. I remember flashes of cops chasing me, but the whole picture was a blur. When this cop told me what I had done, I wanted to kill myself. I reached for the officer's gun and he held me down; all I could do was cry and think of what a horrible person I was. How was I going to explain to this boy's mother that I took her son? I just wanted to die; I became out of control in the hospital to the point where they had to sedate me. After they examined me at the hospital, they released me to the police department, but during my time spent at the hospital, I saw my family there, my mother crying and father in disbelief and my oldest son was really disappointed and mad at me. He didn't even acknowledge me; my daughter and my middle son and boyfriend were hurting and sad more than anything, and even with me lying on that bed, I started to think of drugs—how was I going to get through this without them. I asked my mom to go get me my suboxone because I knew I was going to jail and that would help get through a couple days before I got sick. I convinced my mother that I was in so much pain, I needed them until finally she brought them to me. As they loaded me in the transport unit to go to county jail, I took my first strip. As I drove that forty-five-minute drive, all I could think about was what I had done and the severity of the situation and how I might be charged with vehicular homicide. Reality started to set in on my way to jail.

As I started to come down from the sedation, I took the last strip I had on me of suboxone. I started to panic again about what was happening. I knew that there was a young man in hospital fighting for his life because of me. I began to cry and beg God to help this kid, as I was in the booking room. As the hours passed, I got more and more emotional. I couldn't stop thinking about the horrible thing I had done. I was so upset with myself, I cried out for God to help me. I desperately started to bargain with God, and I remember these words like it was yesterday. I said, "Lord, if you save this kid, I promise, on my children's lives, I will not touch another drug or another drink as long as I live. I will turn my life around to serve you."

Now my prayers and bargaining went well through the night and through the next day. Then that evening, a security guard walked in with a phone and looked at me and said, "The phone's for you."

I refused to take it; I was so scared that the phone call was going to be them telling me the young man died. The guard said, "You really need to take this," and at that point, I got the phone and put it to my ear. It was my mom, and she said, "Shannon," and I answered with a cracking shaky voice, "Yes."

She responded, "You better get on your knees and start thanking God, because that boy you hit just walked out of the hospital with only scrapes and bruises, they are calling him a miracle."

I fell to the floor and started crying and thanking God. I was so relieved, I just cried for hours, thanking my Father.

Little did I know the hard part was still ahead of me. By the time I got to the back area of county jail, I was in full swing of sickness (malaise). I had already been up for two nights and three days and was so sick. I knew I was fighting demons inside of me. I would go into these seizures and shake uncontrollably. My legs wouldn't stop moving. I would involuntarily jerk repeatedly. Not to mention I was constantly sick to my stomach and could not hold down anything. I had no control of my body. I would hold my Bible so tight, reading and praying, praying for help from the sickness. I would get some relief; it would last for about fifteen to twenty minutes, and this went on for many days.

During this time, some of the girls from the streets I knew would offer their own stash (drugs) just because they saw how bad I was doing; they felt bad for me. I even got to the point of locking myself in the cell because the temptation was too much, the temptation of knowing that I just had to ask, and it would be readily available. I knew if I took another drink or did another drug that I would break the bargain I made with God and he would take my child or my children from me, I would rather die than live with knowing that my child died because of my need for drugs. It was the fear of God that kept me from using. On the tenth day that morning, I went down to the tables wrapped in a blanket with a hot water bottle. I sat down at the table at about 8 in the morning, and one of the girls that was awake just looked at me and said, "You still haven't slept, ha."

I shook my head no. I was on my tenth day of sickness with no sleep.

Then suddenly, I felt what I believe was the Holy Spirit, the touch of God. The sickness was gone, just disappeared! I felt like I was floating like a heaviness was taken off me. I had no worries or cares; all the fear was gone. I felt brand-new like if I was twelve years old again like I had a new body. I jumped up and threw my blanket off me and I ran up and down the stairs throughout the pod (jail) screaming, "I'm back, I'm back."

The girls in the pod yelled back at me, "Shut up."

I ran to my Bible that was on the table and flipped it open. I wanted to thank God. I knew this was all God and this is the verse that I read.

> Fear not the things which thou art about to suffer: behold, the devil is about to cast some of you into prison, that ye may be tried; and ye shall have tribulation ten days. Be thou faithful unto death, and I will give thee the crown of life. (Revelation 2:10)

I knew right then I was saved. God granted me his grace and mercy. From that moment, I made a choice to follow Jesus and tell of his goodness and mercy for the rest of my life.

My Father God saved me, he poured his mercy, grace upon me and gave me another chance. I was overwhelmed with joy and thanksgiving.

My Journey with Father

I finally see clearly now; God removed the blindfold and I see what we are dealing with. Drugs and alcohol are not just mind-altering, they are powerful demonic influences that take us over. Let's be honest with ourselves, it is demonic possession. A lot of us think that if we go around telling people we are demonically possessed or our son or daughter is, they might think we are crazy, right. Well, you're not wrong; this is how our society has shifted from calling what is right wrong and what is wrong right. They have put labels on demonic possession, calling it mental illness. Never in the time Jesus was alive did he ever heal someone one from PTSD or bipolar, it was called demonic possession. Jesus healed two kinds of illness because there are only two kinds: physical and spiritual. For most of us, we cannot understand the power that is in drugs. We don't understand what we are dealing with. These drugs are powerful tools the devil uses against us in our weakness.

These demonic forces tear families apart, they destroy relationships, they hurt others physically and emotionally, and eventually they reach their ultimate goal: they consume us, and we die to our sin. Don't you see we are not only killing ourselves every time we use drugs or alcohol, but we are also hurting someone in the process. This is evilness; that is exactly what the enemy wants for us. To be rendered useless in this war between good and evil. Once rendered useless, we begin to war alongside Satan instead of against him. This will ultimately lead us to eternal damnation, the lake of fire for eternity. We all need to wake up and open our eyes to the spiritual realm around us and the way to do this is to accept Jesus as our Lord and

Savior and ask him for his help; surrender yourself to him. He is the only one that has the supernatural power to defeat Satan. We have been at war since the beginning when God created man, and man took off the tree of knowledge (sin), thus bringing death to the human race. Satan's time is short; he is devouring those he can that do not have Jesus. Without Jesus who already won the battle, we are helpless. We can't fight this kind of evil power; we need the power of Jesus Christ to fight through us so that we may be saved and live with him for eternity!

Once I gave my life to God, I was no longer in bondage, and I found that this whole time in my addiction, I was so deceived. As I sat in county jail for the crimes I committed, I couldn't help but have joy radiating out of me. I was free from the bondage of drugs and alcohol. God began to shape and mold me, and believe me, it was painful, not physical pain, but a spiritual pain, a heartfelt pain. I began to tell other women in jail with me the power and mercy of Christ and what my Jesus could do for them. For the next four weeks, I sat in county jail. I was told that I was probably not going to get out for a while. In fact, I was told that I would probably be going to prison straight from county jail.

During those weeks, I talked with my public defender and my family, preparing them for the worst. We all knew I had very serious charges and that I had little hope in getting out on bond. As the time passed in the county jail, waiting for my day of court to come, I had demonic encounters that would try and lead down a path to sin, but God helped me through those paths of darkness and showed me my weaknesses as he molded me into his own. One of those lessons was on anger; it was also the first vision I received from God. That week in the pod (jail), I was feeling very irritated with one of the girls. She was a younger girl that had an addiction problem and was taking advantage of the other girls. I felt like a protector of that pod. I was in a sense like a mom to the girls. I would help them with food when they came in and try to encourage them with scriptures and my own testimony. This girl would take advantage of all the other girls. She would ask them for their commissary (food and hygiene) and always promise to pay them back but never would.

Until one day, when a friend of mine was very upset, she was tearing up when she told me all the things this girl swindled her out of. It upset me to the point that I lost my temper and reverted to that old me, which was a very dark person I don't ever want to be. I ended up jumping across the table, grabbing the girl by her shirt, and putting my face in her face. I screamed obscenities at her, as spit flew from my mouth. She was so scared, she started to cry; she ran up to her cell where she locked herself in. I felt like I had just done something good. I felt boastful and prideful because I took care of my girls. The rest of the pod saw this and they looked at me like a protector, so they began to taunt this girl. She couldn't come out of her cell in fear of what would happen to her. The other girls threatened her constantly about what would happen if she came out. The feeling of power overtook me, and I didn't see that it was manipulation from the enemy.

A couple days passed, and now it was Friday night; there was a shipment of meth that came into the jail day and a lot the girls were using. A couple of my friends came over to me and wanted to get high. I explained to them that I had changed my life, and I would not be a part of that anymore. That upset them. I think it was because they felt a sense of guilt, and it got stronger when I would not participate.

That night, I was in my cell when I woke up to an evil feeling; something was in the room with me. I could feel it; when I turned in my bed and looked over at the door, I saw a shadow come through the bottom as it made its way up the door. I could see it was evil, a demonic spirit; it had these red eyes with large sharp teeth and claws like a bear. It stared at me with the intent of devouring me. It continued to make its way up the door onto the ceiling toward me. I was frightened but angry at the same time. I rebuked this demon in the name of Jesus, but it wasn't stopping or leaving.

As it approached my bed, it was directly above me; it jumped on top of me. I could feel it now, but I couldn't see it. It was suffocating me, and I was trying to get it off. I called out to God. It seemed like for hours as I struggled and fought with this demon, but God wouldn't answer or come to my aid. Finally, I screamed out "Why,

Lord, why won't you help me? I kept my promise I haven't used. I've been telling the girls of you. Why have you abandoned me?"

Then a voice, not audible but like a telepathic voice in my head that I knew was God, said to me, "It was you that opened the door with your anger, who are you to come against my daughter and talk to her like that?"

And I knew at that moment that I had sinned. It was my anger and hate toward this girl I screamed at, this daughter of God, which was tormenting me. It was my anger that allowed this demon in; it gave the foothold for Satan. Immediately, I saw the girl's terrified face in my mind. I asked God for forgiveness, that heartfelt forgiveness as tears ran down my cheeks in sorrow of what I had done. Suddenly, the demon was gone. I felt it come off me immediately upon asking for forgiveness. There was something else though that happened that night. I received a word from God about what was to come. He told me I would be going to prison. He said prison would be my training ground. He needed to prepare me for the things that were to come. He showed a picture of my hometown and women in black clothing weeping over their dead children. In the front of a Walgreens pharmacy, a pharmacy represents drugs. I believe this vision that I had is about the death from drugs and how many will be consumed by the enemy. This vision had me in tears, for what was to come.

That morning when our cells opened up, I went straight to the woman's cell, the one I yelled at, and I apologized asking her to forgive me. She started to cry and said, "No one has ever asked me to forgive them, thank you, I do forgive you and I'm sorry for what I've done."

God allowed me to see and experience what anger can do and how it can overtake us when we give a foothold to Satan. When we allow anger to consume us, it is opening the door for the demonic to take control. It also allowed me to see that others struggle with demons also; it doesn't make them any less God's children and they need help too from the pain they carry.

The day came for my bond to be set; this would be the day that I would either be let out till my court date or stay in jail. This judge was known in the county jail to be very strict, harder on women. The lawyer told me that basically I didn't have a chance and I'd be staying in jail till my court date. Well, praise the Lord that day came, I was released on a bond. My family put up the bond, and I was able to go home with stipulations: one being I had to wear an ankle monitor. God came to my rescue again; I know this was all part of his plan for me. The lawyer's face when the judge allowed a bond set for me to get out was priceless. Even the lawyer told me that God played a part in this decision for he could not understand how she let me out. Now that I look back, I understand he gave me that time (eight months) with my family to show them that I changed and also to give me hope. God had more in mind though; this was the start of my journey in many lessons that would come.

When I was at home for those eight months, I started reading my Bible. I began spending time with the lord. I gave up the cigarettes and started to eat right. I started to take care of my body because I realized that my body was the temple of God. I found that many things we harbor like unforgiveness, resentment, hate, all lead to our destruction. We must learn how to forgive and love, or we will find ourselves right back in bondage to sin. When we experience Christ's gracious forgiveness, we receive peace. To retain this peace, it is necessary to forgive others. Jesus tells us in Matthew 6:14–15, "For if ye forgive men their trespasses, your heavenly Father will also forgive you. But if ye forgive not men their trespasses, neither will your Father forgive your trespasses."

God showed me the freedom that comes from forgiveness. I had to learn to forgive those that have hurt me. It was hard to let the things that have been done to us that are so hurtful and full of hate go, but it is what we are called to do as Christ's followers. I forgave those officers that came against me and hurt me, and in it, I found a freedom that allowed Jesus to remove all the depression, resentment, bitterness, and pain that I was harboring. In this, I have now found that when we give it to God, he is our Defender; he brings about our justice. I now have a great relationship with the police department and all those in the justice system. I have found that all of us, including those in our justice system, deal with our own demons. We must learn to forgive and let go and let God handle it.

Jesus told a story that teaches us about the perils of unforgiveness. The story was about a king who wanted to check his servants' accounts. He found that he had a servant who owed him a very large sum of money, equal to many years' wages. The king told the servant that he, his family, and all his possessions would have to be sold. The servant begged for mercy and the king forgave him of his debt. This servant later found one of his fellow servants who owed him a small sum, about a day's wages. He told his fellow servant that he would have to pay in full. His fellow servant begged for mercy, but the servant would not forgive the debt. When the king heard of this, he called his servant to him. He said, "I forgave you when you asked me. Should you not have done the same?" The king then sent him to prison until the debt could be paid. Jesus then said that our Heavenly Father will not forgive us if we do not forgive others (Matthew 18:23–35).

Hating someone, holding an offense, or harboring a grudge causes many negative effects. The person who allows such attitudes in his life becomes miserable. His health suffers, as do his relationships.

When we don't forgive others, it brings about a bondage to our souls that could be compared to being enslaved by people or bound by a substance addiction. This unforgiveness causes bitterness within us. It locks in sorrow, anger, and strife; it locks out joy, love, and fellowship. This bitterness is a result of a proud spirit that seeks to keep score and gain revenge for perceived and real wrongs. If we refuse to release our offended feelings, they will eventually control us. We will be in bondage to them as well as in the bondage of sin before God. Jesus taught that the only way for us to grant forgiveness to others is in the way He has forgiven us. We are to forgive regardless of the nature or gravity of the offense against us, the number of offenses, or the character of the offender. We are to show unconditional mercy as God has shown mercy to us. As we humble ourselves and extend forgiveness to others, God opens the way for us to seek forgiveness for our own mistakes and sins. God fully forgives all who come to Him with a humble and repentant spirit.

As we follow the Holy Spirit, we will know the truth, and the truth will make us free.

John 8:36 says, "And ye shall know the truth, and the truth shall make you free."

While it is said, "To-day if ye shall hear his voice, Harden not your hearts, as in the provocation" (Hebrews 3:15).

In Matthew 11:28, Jesus said, "Come unto me, all ye that labor and are heavy laden, and I will give you rest." As we follow these teachings, we will be forgiven and will be able to forgive others.

THE ORIGIN OF DECEPTION THROUGH DRUGS

Since the start of mankind, fallen angels roamed the earth; these angels came from the heavenly kingdom, but because they followed Lucifer and waged war against God, they were cast unto earth. These angels saw that the daughters of men were beautiful and went against God and had intercourse with them. They also taught them things like magic, sorcery, which is the use of pharmacia, how to make weapons of war, and other things. This is where drug use all began; it was to show man how to call upon spirits to do their bidding and open up the spiritual realms. Throughout the Bible, we hear about sorcery, witchcraft, divination, among other things and how it is a sin; in fact, in the Old Testament when God chose Israel to be his chosen people, any of them caught practicing these occult things would be put to death.

Once Jesus came, he came as our salvation for all men that whosoever believed in him would not perish but have everlasting life (John 3:16). These words are true on the basis that we give up our sin and take up the cross, leaving behind the life of sin and renewing our lives in Jesus. By living a righteous life of obedience to God. For when we obey our Father, we show our love for him.

Taking a look at the drugs commonly used today, we know that a lot of them have been used in Shamanism, witchcraft, and pagan religions to contact spirits and gods that the Bible teaches are demons. Although the initial effects of these drugs are different, they all cause similar negative symptoms including panic attacks, anxiety, paranoia, mood swings, suicidal tendencies, hallucinations, violent tendencies, and out-of-body experiences. The reason these symptoms are common to all types of drugs is they are symptoms of demonic influence.

The symptoms of demonic influence are no mystery. They have been observed and documented for thousands of years. The best source for understanding how demons affect people is the Bible. It attributes irrational fear, violent tendencies, antisocial tendencies, sexual perversion, dishonesty, suicide psychic abilities, and superhuman strength to demons.

Christian ministers and researchers have observed these symptoms as well as others. Dr. Kurt Koch documented six hundred cases of demonization through involvement in witchcraft and the symptoms he observed they included: abnormal sexuality, violent tempers, belligerence, tendencies to addiction, emotional disturbance, compulsive thoughts, depression, suicidal thoughts, anxiety disorders, destructive urges, fits of mania, tendency toward violent acts and crime, anti-Christian bigotry, false piety, blasphemous thoughts, and religious delusions.

The people that Dr. Kosh ministered to were not using drugs, but the symptoms he documented are common among drug users. His research is therefore consistent with the Bible teaching that drug use is Sorcery! The biblical view of drug use is also supported by other Christian researchers. Elizabeth Hillstrom wrote a book called *Testing the Spirits'*. She examined the spiritual practices of the New Age movement. She found that those who practice Eastern Style meditation, chanting, astral projection, yoga, transcendental meditation, and spirit channeling often suffered from anxiety, depression, mood swings, panic attacks, antisocial behavior, and anti-Christian sentiments. The New Age practices are actually very old forms of witchcraft and idolatry, and they are performed to alter the consciousness in order to commune with demonic gods and spirits. The fact that they cause symptoms seen in drug users is consistent with our view that drug use is a type of witchcraft and idolatry.

Fifty years of scientific research has confirmed the validity of the biblical view of drug use. Thousands of studies have found that drug users suffer from anxiety, apathy, blackouts, depression, flashbacks, hallucinations, mood swings, out-of-body experiences, obsessive-compulsive behavior, panic attacks, paranoia, suicidal tendencies, superhuman strength, and violent tendencies as we are about to see these are all demonic influences.

Researchers and psychiatrists consider the symptoms of drug use to be a result of psychosis rather than demons, but many of the symptoms of psychosis are symptoms of demonic influence with different more scientific names. Those who have out-of-body experiences are said to have "depersonalization disorder," Those who experience blackouts are diagnosed with "dissociative amnesia." Those who suffer mood swings have "bipolar disorder," those who experience panic attacks and paranoia have "anxiety disorder," those who commit suicide have "suicidal behavior disorder," and those with religious delusions have "delusional disorder." These symptoms are not new; they have been around for thousands of years associated with demonic influence.

Once we understand that the symptoms of drug-induced psychosis are symptoms of demonic influence, we realize that all scientific research on drug use supports what the Bible teaches. The American Manual of Mental Disorder (DSM-V) supports biblical view of drug use. When it describes conditions such as "opioid-induced psychotic disorder with hallucinations" and "cannabis-induced anxiety disorder," it confirms that drug use leads to demonic influence because hallucinations and anxiety are common symptoms of demonic influence.

We have all been deceived since the late 1800 when mental illness was introduced, and God was taken out of the picture. The only way they could explain these bursts of rage and delusions, talking to oneself was a diagnosis of mental illness. In fact, most mental illness is demonic possession, but it was explained away when evolution came into the picture no God, no devil, no such thing as demonic possession. Only problem is there was and still is demonic possession. Throughout history and throughout the Bible, it talks about possession no more than two thousand years ago. When we look at the horrific actions taken by people while under the influence, there is no other explanation than demonic. I have stories of moms telling me that they killed their children while under the influence of drugs, because they thought their child was possessed by a demon or Satan himself. A man who raped and killed a two-month-old baby while high on meth, yet he doesn't even remember the incident and the stories go on and on. This is not human behavior, a human being in their right mind would never do this. When Jesus came, he cast out the demons and it continued with his followers: The following is from Mark 5:–17:

> And they came to the other side of the sea, into the country of the Gerasenes. And when he was come out of the boat, straightway there met him out of the tombs a man with an unclean spirit, who had his dwelling in the tombs: and no man could any more bind him, no, not with a chain; because that he had been often bound with fetters and chains, and the chains had been rent asunder by him, and the fetters broken in pieces: and no man had strength to tame him. And always, night and day, in the tombs and in the mountains, he was crying out, and cutting himself with stones. And when he saw Jesus from afar, he ran and worshipped him; and crying out with a loud voice, he saith, What have I to do with thee, Jesus, thou Son of the Most High God? I adjure thee by God, torment me not. For he said unto him, Come forth, thou unclean spirit, out of the man. And he asked him, What is thy name? And he saith unto him, My name is Legion; for we are many. And he besought him much that he would not send them away out of the country. Now there was there on the mountain side a great herd of swine feeding. And they besought him, saying, send us into the swine, that we may enter into them. And he gave them leave. And the unclean spirits came out, and entered into the swine: and the herd rushed down the steep into

the sea, *in number* about two thousand; and they were drowned in the sea. And they that fed them fled, and told it in the city, and in the country. And they came to see what it was that had come to pass. And they come to Jesus, and behold him that was possessed with demons sitting, clothed and in his right mind, *even* him that had the legion: and they were afraid. And they that saw it declared unto them how it befell him that was possessed with demons, and concerning the swine. And they began to beseech him to depart from their borders.

First thing that this scripture shows us is that it doesn't matter how demonized someone is, Jesus can save them instantly.

We also see that demons are dark forces that have four characteristics of personality: mind, will, emotion, and the ability to communicate. First, the demons knew who Jesus was (mind). They wanted to go into the pigs (will). They were afraid of Jesus (emotion). And they begged him not to torture them (communication). They also have personal names (Legion).

A demon has personalities, but they are still spirits and lack a physical body. When they enter a human, they recruit a new body for the kingdom of Satan. They also gain a physical body they use to carry out the schemes and tactics of Satan. This man had many demons inside of him, and they had complete control of him. They controlled him physically. (They had him run naked through the tombs and cut himself.) This is the shame and torture Satan wants to do to humans. They controlled what he said. (They spoke through him.) They also controlled what he thought. (After Jesus cast them out, the man was "in his right mind.") The demon in this man was working for Satan, but demons are creatures, and as such, they are ultimately subject to their creator. Notice that they never question or challenge Jesus's authority over them. As soon as the demons saw Jesus, the man fell to his knees and they begged Jesus not to torture them, nor could they do anything Jesus did not allow them to do.

The name Legion is an indication of the number of demons that were in this man. A Roman army legion consists of six thousand soldiers! An enormous number of demons were dwelling in the Gerasene, and he was obviously severely demonized. As what was shown earlier on signs of demonic influence this type of behavior is the exception not the rule, and nevertheless the violent tendencies, superhuman strength, nakedness, and self-mutilation seen in the Gerasene are also seen in drug users today. This is consistent with our understanding of pharmacia, witchcraft, sorcery, and it shows us that some people become severely demonized when they use drugs.

There is nowhere in the Bible that says demons would go away and there would be no more possession. On the contrary, Jesus warned us about the last days that Satan would be raging war on the saints; he can't rage war without an army. If they could possess people, then they can possess people now. Because of our ignorance and blindness, we can't see what is happening all around us. Our government would never admit that there is demon possession. It would destroy their honey pot of big pharma, all the money they make off prescription drugs to treat depression, anxiety, mental illness, physical illness, and pain. The list goes on and on when all they need is Jesus. Jesus can destroy your demons; they have no authority in your life when you accept him and trust him. He actually blesses you with the authority to cast demons out through his power; isn't that awesome?

If big pharma, government, and those 1 percent that make up the world's money can keep people in the dark and ignorant, they will have total control; we must wake up. We are at war, a spiritual war that has been going on since the beginning of time. Just because we don't see doesn't mean it doesn't exist, and we see it all around us. People just don't understand or are too busy with their own agenda to recognize what is happening in their own families to their own children. Children now live in a world where acceptance of evil is rampant. It has been programmed in our society; we have been desensitized to sin. We are told we must accept one another for who they are, though the Bible teaches us to clearly stay away from people that live in sin. Do you see how they have twisted everything for an agenda against the very word of God? Now we fear the things our government and the media tell us to fear instead of fearing God when in the Bible it tells us, "Say to them that are of a fearful heart, Be strong, fear not: behold, your God will come *with* vengeance, *with* the recompense of God; he will come and save you" (Isaiah 35:4).

"The fear of man bringeth a snare; But whoso putteth his trust in Jehovah shall be safe" (Proverbs 29:25).

"In nothing be anxious; but in everything by prayer and supplication with thanksgiving let your requests be made known unto God. And the peace of God, which passeth all understanding, shall guard your hearts and your thoughts in Christ Jesus" (Philippians 4:6–7).

"Have not I commanded thee? Be strong and of good courage; be not affrighted, neither be thou dismayed: for Jehovah thy God is with thee whithersoever thou goest" (Joshua 1:9).

Believing in Christ is the best way to deal with anxiety and fear. We know that he is with us forever. This can calm our hearts in the middle of an emotional storm. He is our comfort that we run to our place of safety.

God gave us a manual on how to live life with rules to follow, and when we do not follow those rules, we step out of his protection and open ourselves up to sin, which then can overcome us to the point of demonic possession. Drugs take us to another level of demonic possession because there is a power that we do not know about. A supernatural power that requires a supernatural power to defeat it. All souls eventually reap what they sow, and the repeated practice of drug use (narcotics) will eventually result in the user being exposed to the supernatural power of demons. Their power may manifest within the user or from without, but it will come. When it does, the user will experience one or more of the following symptoms: violent tendencies, superhuman strength, panic attacks, paranoia, mood swings, suicidal tendencies, sexual immorality, obsessive compulsive disorder, flashbacks, apathy, blackouts, hallucinations, out-of-body-experiences.

People today do not understand the ramifications of using drugs; they do not understand it is the practice of sorcery, witchcraft, pharmacia. Because they do not know God, if they knew God, their eyes would be open to the attacks of the enemy. Sadly, the world had pushed God out, out of our classrooms, out of our justice systems, even out of our homes and out of our lives. We have instead been deceived into bringing in Hollywood to entertain us, which is a tactic of Satan, a desensitizing to our natural order of living holy. Instead, it shows people that sin is the way we are supposed to live. Hollywood says, "It's not sin, it's the way of life and God understands and accepts us because he is all about love and will accept us sinning against him." This is wrong over and over; in the Bible, God teaches that sin leads death, eternal damnation, the lake of fire in hell. In fact, God explicitly tells us in the Bible to choose the way of the world or his way, but you can't be both and if you chose the world, you are an enemy of God.

God expects Christians to be just like Jesus (1 John 4:17), who was primarily focused on accomplishing Father God's will, but many of us are now focused on our own agendas, forgetting that we are called to be God's ambassadors (2 Corinthians 5:20).

First Corinthians 6:19–20 reads: "Have not I commanded thee? Be strong and of good courage; be not affrighted, neither be thou dismayed: for Jehovah thy God is with thee whithersoever thou goest."

But how many of us continue to change our view and align them with the world on issues such as abortion, homosexuality, marriage, and many other pressing matters? How many of us have become ashamed of God's righteous standards?

In Mark 8:38, Jesus said, "For whosoever shall be ashamed of me and of my words in this adulterous and sinful generation, the Son of man also shall be ashamed of him, when he cometh in the glory of his Father with the holy angels."

We must focus on God's will instead of what the world is doing. The world follows its own compulsive nature, but the Bible warns against this in Romans 12:2, when it states: "And be not fashioned according to this world: but be ye transformed by the renewing of your mind, that ye may prove what is the good and acceptable and perfect will of God."

If you conform and change your thought process to suit what the world is doing, you won't even understand God's will because the world is in opposition to his views. In a spiritual view, which would be the equivalent of oil trying to mix with water. It's just not possible.

Second Corinthians 6:14 in the Amplified Bible reads, "Be not unequally yoked with unbelievers: for what fellowship have righteousness and iniquity? Or what communion hath light with darkness?" In other words, do not make mismatched alliances with them, inconsistent with your faith. "For what partnership can righteousness have with lawlessness? Or what fellowship can light have with darkness?"

The kingdom of heaven is advancing, and, with it, the Word of God is permeating the hearts of believers and realigning how they think, act, and the results they ultimately get. All the while, the world is growing more depraved as it follows Satan's alternative view.

This is an important moment in time for all of us that call ourselves Christians to really take inventory of ourselves. Do your views line up with God's character and his mindset or the world's? The Bible says you will surely be on one side or the other.

As a born-again Christian, I can say that the life I led was of sin. I was engulfed in it drugs, lies, deceit, sexual immorality, the list goes on and on. When my walk with God began, he began to mold and shape me in his way. Eventually, I found that I had that spirit that he promises when we follow him a spirit of power, love, and self-discipline. Many people nowadays are lost in their pain, feeling unloved that they turn to drugs, sex, material possessions—whatever makes them feel somewhat alive. Problem is that it's just a temporary fix for a moment that is lost in time. We keep chasing after those moments to bring us short-lived happiness when the whole time Jesus is waiting for us to reach out to him to give us everlasting joy. In our world today, homosexuality is rampant, and according to the world, we are to accept this new normal of men identifying as women, women identifying as men. Men having sexual relations with men and woman having sexual relations with woman. The problem here is that homosexuality is sin according to the word of God. These are not my words but God's.

> Or know ye not that the unrighteous shall not inherit the kingdom of God? Be not deceived: neither fornicators, nor idolaters, nor adulterers, nor effeminate, nor abusers of themselves with men, nor thieves, nor covetous, nor drunkards, nor revilers, nor extortioners, shall inherit the kingdom of God. (1 Corinthians 6:9–10)

> For fornicators, for abusers of themselves with men (Homosexuality), for men stealers, for liars, for false swearers, and if there be any other thing contrary to the sound doctrine. (1 Timothy 1:10)

But we love these people. Why because Father tells us to love the person, hate the sin. It is our duty as Christians though to let them know that it is sin that they are practicing; you plant the seed and allow God to grow it in their hearts. As a former drug addict, I identify with the sexual sin that comes with that life. We all have fallen short of sexual sin. No one is perfect in this area. Whether physically done it or mentally thought about it, it is still sin.

Jesus said in Mathew 5:27–28, "Ye have heard that it was said, Thou shalt not commit adultery: but I say unto you, that every one that looketh on a woman to lust after her hath committed adultery with her already in his heart." I understand though that people are looking for love, for someone to love them. And in so many cases of homosexuality, they turn to the same sex because the opposite sex hurt them deeply and they feel as though they can never trust them again. Others identify with the same sex better thus feeling attraction toward them. Women know what makes another woman feel better or how to please them, right. This goes for men also. Problem is that God made a woman for a man to be fruitful and bring about Godly offspring. Women and men joined together in marriage, as it was meant to be from the beginning with Adam and Eve, because they bring something that the other doesn't have.

Let me explain, we affirm God's design for the two sexes—male and female—and believe that each is a glorious gift from God. Our sexuality is meant to be offered back to Him. For some, this means joining in a one-man, one-woman marriage—for procreation, union, and mutual delight. For others, this means celibacy, which allows for undivided devotion to Christ. Sexual expression is designed for the marital relationship, and homosexual lust and behavior are among the sexual sins that are outside God's created intent and desire for us.

Because we are deeply concerned about the hearts and souls of those who identify themselves as "gay, lesbian, or bisexual," we want those men and women to know that God loves them with an ever-lasting love. Through salvation and the work of the Holy Spirit, God can empower them to live according to his design and standards for sexuality. He offers the grace to accept their true identity—not as gay, lesbian, or bisexual—but as his sons and daughters, embracing their biological reality as male or female.

God knew you before the foundations of the earth were made. He does not make mistakes; he is perfection as is his work. This means that he knew what and who you were to be on this earth (male, female). You are his masterpiece, created perfectly to live out according to his will, but along the way, we started living according to our will. God loves us and wants us to be part of his kingdom. He gave us instructions on how to live life and not taste death. Instead, we live our lives here on earth like there's no tomorrow and forget that this is such a short time compared to eternity. This life is but a glimmering speck, a pebble of sand, compared to rolling hills of endless sand pebbles of eternity. Acceptance into heaven for eternity means turning from your sin, admitting you're a sinner, asking for forgiveness, knowing Jesus died for your sins and rose again, and asking him to have a relationship with you. Jesus is a mystery, and we won't know everything until we get to heaven. We must all follow the example of Jesus and stop our sinning, for we cannot continue on in our sin and be joined with Father for eternity.

> Flee fornication. Every sin that a man doeth is without the body; but he that commit-teth fornication sinneth against his own body. (1 Corinthians 6:18)

Let marriage *be* had in honor among all, and *let* the bed *be* undefiled: for fornicators and adulterers God will judge. (Hebrews 13:4)

For this is the will of God, your sanctification: that you abstain from sexual immorality; that each one of you know how to control his own body in holiness and honor, not in the passion of lust like the Gentiles who do not know God. (1 Thessalonians 4:3–5)

But I say to you that everyone who looks at a woman with lustful intent has already committed adultery with her in his heart. (Matthew 5:27–28)

But sexual immorality and all impurity or covetousness must not even be named among you, as is proper among saints. (Ephesians 5:3)

No temptation has overtaken you that is not common to man. God is faithful, and he will not let you be tempted beyond your ability, but with the temptation he will also provide the way of escape, that you may be able to endure it. (1 Corinthians 10:13)

Now the works of the flesh are evident: sexual immorality, impurity, sensuality. (Galatians 5:19)

But because of the temptation to sexual immorality, each man should have his own wife and each woman her own husband. (1 Corinthians 7:2)

> Put to death therefore what is earthly in you: sexual immorality, impurity, passion, evil desire, and covetousness, which is idolatry. (Colossians 3:5)

> For this is the will of God, your sanctification: that you abstain from sexual immorality. (1 Thessalonians 4:3)

> For you may be sure of this, that everyone who is sexually immoral or impure, or who is covetous (that is, an idolater), has no inheritance in the kingdom of Christ and God. (Ephesians 5:5)

> We must not indulge in sexual immorality as some of them did, and twenty-three thousand fell in a single day. (1 Corinthians 10:8)

When we understand that it is in our nature to sin, that Satan appeals to make us obedient to our sinful pleasures instead of God and that this world is filled with temptations to sin, we then can understand why we need Jesus. When we become reborn in Jesus, we are able to overcome sin, we can resist temptation from the world around us. When we are reborn in Jesus, we are free from sin's bondage. Jesus cleanses us from our sins and makes us righteous in the eyes of God. God then gives us the Holy Spirit so that we can fulfill the acts of outwardly and inwardly righteousness according to God's law. God enables us to fulfill this covenant with his Grace and mercy. This covenant not only allows us to know God intimately, but it is also a covenant wherein we can obey the law of Christ because we know him, and he writes his law upon our hearts. It is important to understand that the covenant with God is not just about forgiveness but about obedience. God tell us this in scripture:

> I will give you a new heart and put a new spirit in you: I will remove from you your heart of stone and give you a heart of flesh. I will put my spirit

in you and move you to follow my decrees and be
careful to keep my laws. (Ezekiel 36:26–27)

I tell you the truth, no one can enter the kingdom
of God unless he is born of water and the spirit.
Flesh gives birth to flesh, but the spirit gives birth
to the spirit. You should not be surprised at my
saying, "You must be born again." (John 3:5–7)

Once we have received this free gift of forgiveness of our sins
and our free spiritual rebirth and the gift of knowing God and the
power to do his will through his Son Jesus Christ, we can obey God.
We can please God and live our lives according to his commands
by his grace and through our faith. And what is even more is God
gives us the power to stop using drugs. He changes our hearts, so we
no longer want to do them. We get freedom from the desire to use
drugs, a newfound freedom from our Savior.

When we come to know God, we don't want to sin anymore;
we want to please our Father because of our love for him. We are
still tempted by Satan, but we are able to resist through the power of
Jesus. When we do fall short because we are human and sin is among
us, we as children of God hate that we have disobeyed. Conviction
and remorse over the sin is hard to experience, but it is a good thing;
it means we are being chastised (punished) for our sin because we are
God's children. It shows our desire to please God and that God has
indeed given us a new heart that desires to obey him.

Demon Possession through Drugs and Alcohol

The majority of people's understanding does not include demon possession when getting high and/or drunk. In fact, we look at getting high as an escape from our problems or the way the world has portrayed it where alcohol and drugs is what fun is all about. It is a way to feel better when we have suffered a loss of opportunity or grieving of a loved one that has left our lives. It is something we do with our friends to have a good time. We collate drugs and alcohol with having fun, grieving, and medicinally for our pains physically and emotionally.

In all reality, drugs and alcohol are what causes our misguidedness to true joy. Our lives become chaotic, sorrowful, and unmanageable and we fall deeper into the trap Satan has set for us. We have opened the door for Satan to wreak havoc even to the point of our own death or the death of another.

Some factual examples I'm going to share are of people that have been using drugs and have gone into an altered state of mind where the demons were able to take control (demon possession)

A young man that overdosed on bath salts described his experience in an interview with CNN He said, "It felt so evil like the darkest evilest thing imaginable." He said initially he felt "ten feet tall and bulletproof," but when his trip went bad, he became paranoid and felt fear and darkness. He said he felt impending doom was coming down on him. He said, "I felt like I was about to bust loose and hurt somebody." Now this man was able to resist the urge to hurt somebody. Not all bath salt users go through this, although some acts of violence are so irrational the only way to explain it is demonic because human beings could not do these things.

Marijuana users have had this spiritual experience according to Charles D. Tart that interviewed some college kids:

> One in five agreed with this statement: "I have lost all control and had been taken over by an outside force or will that have a hostile or evil intent for a while."
>
> Meanwhile these are the statements made from these kids during the study:
>
> I feel more in contact with the spirits.
> I feel in touch with a higher power.
> I felt located outside of my physical body.
> I can foretell the future by a type of precognition.
>
> All of these statements are common occult practices to call upon evil spirits.

As a former pot smoker, I can confirm that memory loss and a motivational syndrome are real. I also know that marijuana can put you in contact with demons, if pot was not potent enough to enable contacts with spirits. Shamans and Sadhus wouldn't use marijuana, they use it explicitly for this purpose.

During a drug-induced high of meth, a young man killed a two-month-old baby after he sexually mutilated her. He could not remember himself doing this or even fathom the thought and eventually hung himself in prison.

Two friends decided to take mushrooms on one given day, and one of the friends found himself in an alternate reality where he perceived the friend as Satan and himself as God. In this battle he perceived as reality, he ripped out the heat of his friend and then peeled off the skin on his face. He really believed he was defeating Satan and doing the right thing. When he came to, he was in utter horror of what he had done and is now serving a life sentence.

These are just a few instances of the horrific things people do and or encounter under the influence of drugs and alcohol. Then there are those who believe that because they are on a prescription from a doctor, it is okay, but if it is a narcotic pain and or for mental disorder, you may want to rethink what it is you're really depending on, God or the drug.

The reason that prescription drug abuse has become an epidemic is because of the misuse. Many people start using them for legitimate pain, but then they become dependent. Now the body gets more pain because the need for the drug increases. The drug becomes the cause of the pain when it was supposed to be the cure. Now more and more are needed to get to that level of pain management. In all truth, once the body is detoxed of these pain medications, it heals and the pain subsides. Many people don't understand that a prescribed narcotic is a drug; just because it is a prescription does not make it any less dangerous than heroin on the streets. In fact, oxycodone is a pure form of opiate whereas heroin is a cut product of opiate. This is why the overdose deaths on ox's in our country is at an all-time high. The other prescription medication fentanyl is a synthetic opioid that is 80 to 100 times stronger than morphine. Pharmaceutical fentanyl was developed for pain management. The fentanyl now that is being mass produced into prescription medication is alarming. We are seeing a huge jump in overdoses. These prescription medications are being sold through the internet and on the streets, containing lethal doses of fentanyl.

When people start taking these drugs for pleasure and abusing them, they move out of the realm of medicine into the realm of sorcery (pharmacia).

God wants us to depend on him and him alone for comfort. When we put drugs as a priority in our life to function, they become an idol, and that is idolatry.

God should come first in our lives, and if he is not, that is a sin.

If you are a user, please think about these following questions and how they pertain in your own life.

1. What is the first thing you think of when you wake? Is it drugs?
2. Is your drug habit causing pain in your life to you or others?
3. Are you not being able to meet your costs of living because you are spending your money on drugs?
4. Are you able to function (do daily routine) without the drug?

If your answer was yes to any of these questions, you are in bondage to a demonic spirit.

The good news is that we have a Savior that is more powerful than any demonic spirit. He already overcame the ultimate battle with Satan and is waiting to give you victory over your demons. We just have to call upon him and surrender. Let Jesus take the wheel.

MENTAL ILLNESS CAN BE A PHYSICAL ISSUE

We know that one of the consequences of the fall is the corruption of God's good and perfect creation of our bodies (2 Cor. 4:16; 1 Cor. 15:42; Psa. 73:26; Isa. 40:30). Our earthly lives are limited, and eventually, our bodies will fail us. This also applies to our minds. Throughout Scripture, we see biblical figures such as David (Psa. 38:4), Job (Job 3:26), Elijah (1 Kings 19:4), and Jonah (Jonah 4:3) dealing with deep feelings of despair, anger, depression, and loneliness. While some of these things can be attributed to spiritual warfare, it can be of a physical nature. Since we know that our bodies are prone to go awry at times, it's possible that what we are experiencing is related to chemical imbalances or other things happening within our brains.

If this is the case, Jesus gives an example of how we should care for one's physical needs in the parable of the Good Samaritan. When the Samaritan comes across the badly injured man on the side of the road, he takes him to be bandaged and cared for until he recovers (Luke 10:34). Other places throughout Scripture show God's people using elements from the earth such as leaves and figs to assist in the healing process from physical ailments (Ezekiel 47:12; 1 Tim. 5:23; Isaiah 38:21). Perhaps, in some cases, our depression, anxiety, or any other thing that we would consider to be mental illness may have a connection to our disobedience and sin toward God. While we know that those who have placed their trust in Christ have freedom from condemnation for their sins (Rom. 8:1), we may experience its earthly consequences. When we are confronted with the brokenness of ourselves and our sin, the conviction may be overwhelming and give us feelings of grief and despair. We see this take place when David is confronted with his affair with Bathsheba and the murder of her husband (Psa. 51; 1 Kings 12). We also see characters where their mental state is somehow connected to their spiritual state (Dan. 4:28-33; 1 Sam. 16:14). Lastly, there are numerous accounts where the spiritual and physical seem to be connected, such as the account of Legion in the New Testament (Mark 5:1–20; Luke 8:26–39). From these examples, the hope we have in the midst of mental suffering is that the Lord knows, hears, can heal, and is always ready to forgive our sins when we come to him (1 John 1:9).

OBEDIENCE IS LOVE

"God sent his only begotten son for whosoever believe shall not perish but have everlasting life" (John 3:16).

This is God's love for us. God is all powerful; there is nothing he cannot do, and that problem you are experiencing whether it be drugs, alcohol, homosexuality, transgender, pornography, gambling, whatever sin it is, nothing is too big for God. It is important to understand when we give our lives to God and accept Jesus Christ, we become reborn.

God says: "I will give you a new heart and put a new spirit in you: I will remove from you your heart of stone and give you a heart of flesh. And I will put my spirit in you and move you to follow my decrees and be careful to follow my laws" (Ezekiel 36:26–27).

The born-again believer is given a new heart and mind and attitude toward God. We are given the desire to please him, and the Holy Spirit enables us to do so by empowering us to say no to sin and yes to Jesus's commands. The ultimate reason God does all this for us is no to make us good enough to go to heaven or to keep us from going to hell. He does this for his love for us. Those who respond to the love God has to offer through Jesus are blessed with the ability to obey God so that we can love him in return.

Our love for God is shown through our obedience to him. When we love someone or something, we do everything in our power to please them; this is the same when we love God.

Now that we have identified the problem and we know why we are experiencing what drugs actually do which is open us up to demonic entities. We can start to build our strategy.

SURRENDER

O nce we understand that there is a power greater than we can imagine holding us in bondage. Then we can know that the only way out is by accepting Jesus Christ as our Lord and Savior, admitting to God that we need his help and receiving it. It is free, for God sent his son for you and me for this purpose that we may have freedom through Jesus. He is the only one powerful enough to save you from this evil that has you captive.

TAKE OFF THE OLD

Let go of your old self, let it die, and begin to experience the new you through Christ. Allow him to mold and shape you in his righteousness; this is not easy, my friend. In fact, it is one of the hardest steps, but let me tell you it is well worth the journey. For God says, "Turn to me and I shall show you great and mighty things, things you do not know of." Walking in righteousness does not mean we have to be perfect for we are merely human. But with Christ, all things are possible. Even you, my friend, are called to be part of the church, the church of Christ, for Jesus is our cornerstone. God tells us, "For many are called but few will answer." Will you be the one that answers the call?

Taking off our old self means no more drugs, alcohol, or mind-altering substances. Once we are clear minded and have our wits about us, then we can identify the attacks of the enemy. We can identify the sin in our lives, as we put on the righteousness of Christ. This is where God shows us we need to make changes. One of my struggles in learning to let go of my old self was being able to tear down the wall of resentment and anger I had. For this was just one of the many struggles I went through when learning why I used drugs and alcohol, and a lot of doctors will diagnose you with PTSD just as they did me.

You see, I blamed my usage on the justice system and on my past. I used because of the hurt they inflicted on me both mentally and physically; that was my thinking. This was the deception and manipulation Satan planted in my mind. I was played like a violin and then called it PTSD. So that I could have an excuse to use, "I have PTSD I need to use" or "You don't understand this is the only thing that calls me down, I need it." Hence the word *need*. You don't need drugs and or alcohol. Satan wants you to believe you do so that you cannot get close to God, and he can keep you his puppet, but God tells us to come to him for he is enough. "Do not fear for I am with you, do not be in dismay. I will help you and strengthen you and I will uphold you in my mighty right hand" (Isaiah 41:10). My resentment for the police and my past experiences had me living in a world of anger, bitterness, resentment, and unforgiveness. Every time I would get high or drunk, my anger would then really come out.

Now I understand though that it wasn't me, but a demonic spirit that used me to destroy others and myself. I'm sure if you're a user, you have experienced blackouts. Why do you think you can't remember? They're blackouts and we are told to believe this happened to all of us when we get wasted; we logically tell ourselves that it happens to everyone, and it becomes a joke. We don't understand the seriousness behind this. You see, when you black out, a demonic force takes over your body and tries to shame you. Sometimes, it can even go so far and kill you or hurt someone around you. This also can happen with anger. How many times can you remember when you got so angry, that you just saw red and could not stop? I know it's happened to me, and I have hurt someone to the point that they could have died, and I would be in prison. Anger is also a demonic spirit that we must take off ourselves and the only way is through Christ. We have to forgive and turn the other cheek; otherwise, the enemy will use this to destroy us and our relationship with God. Forgiveness is letting go and giving it to God.

Sometimes, we fall to sin, and this is where we need to get closer to God and let him show us where we got deceived. God is not expecting us to be perfect that would be impossible. Only one has ever been perfect, that is Jesus. By walking with God daily, praying, and reading his word, we can certainly get close to his perfection. It means turning to righteousness and staying away from evil. Sometimes, it takes walking away from a loved one because you cannot participate in sin with them any longer. We must tear down our house (life) we have built of sin and rebuild with Jesus as the foundation.

Where did we go wrong?

It wasn't where we went wrong, but where society led us into believing it is about the environment that we grew up in and the influences around us that are wrong that go against God and teach us that sin is the norm, and farther and farther, we distance ourselves from God until society pushes God out altogether. In Mark 4, Jesus talks about the environment we are planted in:

THE PARABLE OF THE SOWER

Again, Jesus began to teach by the lake. The crowd that gathered around him was so large that he got into a boat and sat in it out on the lake, while all the people were along the shore at the water's edge. He taught them many things by parables, and in his teaching said: "Listen! A farmer went out to sow his seed. As he was scattering the seed, some fell along the path, and the birds came and ate it up. Some fell on rocky places, where it did not have much soil. It sprang up quickly, because the soil was shallow. But when the sun came up, the plants were scorched, and they withered because they had no root. Other seed fell among thorns, which grew up and choked the plants, so that they did not bear grain. Still other seed fell on good soil. It came up, grew and produced a crop, some multiplying thirty, some sixty, some a hundred times. "Then he said anyone with ears should listen and understand.

Then Jesus said to them, "Don't you understand this parable? How then will you understand any parable? The farmer sows the word. Some people are like seed along the path, where the word is sown. As soon as they hear it, Satan comes and takes away the word that was sown in them. Others, like seed sown on rocky places, hear the word and at once receive it with joy. But since they have no root, they last only a short time. When trouble or persecution comes because of the word, they quickly fall away. Still others, like seed sown among thorns, hear the word; but the worries of this life, the deceitfulness of wealth and the desires for other things come in and choke the word, making it unfruitful. Others, like seed sown on good soil, hear the word, accept it, and produce a crop—some thirty, some sixty, some a hundred times what was sown."

What seed are you? We need to look at our surroundings; are you listening and understanding where you are planted? If it is not good soil, if you are surrounded with weeds (wickedness), you will be consumed. If you don't have roots in the foundation of Jesus, you're only going to last but a short time and fall back into sin. Don't let the world consume you. Seek God and he will lead you to that fertile soil.

What we don't realize is that we live in an alternate reality; we don't understand what is happening around us. Until we accept Jesus in our lives, then he begins to open our eyes to what is real and what is to come. Spiritual warfare is all around us; good and evil exist and influences our thoughts and our actions. When we use drugs, these demonic evil spirits are able to use us as vessels for their bidding, and anyone that has ever been under the influence more than a couple times could attest to seeing into a spiritual realm or alternate dimension that they can't explain, for example: Sandy, a woman I met in prison, told me she was under the influence of meth, and all night she ran from the devil. She could see him coming after her, and all she knew was to keep running until morning light and she would be safe. She said by morning, she was so exhausted that she collapsed in the middle of the street. Thank God that she did not get run over and someone stopped and called for help.

Another testified that during a weekend of crack cocaine usage, he saw the devil face to face. He was in a dark closet paranoid, and as he lit the lighter to take another hit, the devil appeared to him and blew out the flame. He said that was it, he was done with crack; he stopped smoking crack that night. Unfortunately, he continued with other drugs and has since passed away.

I myself have experienced the demonic influence while in my addiction; there were times that I would black out and do things that were shaming to myself.

There was a time when my own son called my mother because he didn't know what was wrong with Mom; all he knew was it was not me. I was crawling on the floor like an animal speaking gibberish. They my, son, daughter, and mother began to pray for me in the name of Jesus. I then just stood up and went to my room and took a shower. When I came out of the shower, my mom said I was fine, talking to her like normal, and then went to bed. I didn't remember any of this, even when my mom came the next day to ask me what I was on. I couldn't remember her even being there or for that matter what had taken place that night. You see, these blackouts are demonic possessions. When I was taking the cops on that high-speed chase and hit a number of people including a young man on a motorcycle, I blacked out and Satan used me in hurting others. I thank God every day that the boy I hit or anyone else for that matter didn't die. This is no joke. People kill themselves and others while under the influence of drugs and alcohol and don't even remember what horrific thing they did. Because for that moment, they have been used to carry out the demonic orders of Satan to kill, steal, and destroy.

I have seen and witnessed the demonic not only while in prison but also while helping others find God. I have had people ask me to help them because they can't understand what is happening to them. I've seen things while laying hands, praying, and casting out demonic entities that I cannot explain. I know that without a doubt that there is a God and a devil, and we are at war. Humans are in the midst of this war, and the demons hate us. They want to kill us because they have turned from God, and they have no hope of salvation. They are trying to destroy God's children because of the jealousy and hatred they have for us being created in our father's image. Drugs and alcohol are one of the greatest tools of Satan. He is the Father of Lies, and when we fall into his trap of addiction, he gloats and begins to torture us. Keeping us in bondage until our death or until we call upon the Name of Jesus and surrender our lives to him and escape the trap of the devil!

God is our Father, and just like any father and mother, we want what is best for our children. We know that if we do not punish our children, they don't learn a lesson. We must understand that the trials we go through are for us to learn from and become stronger. Not all trials are from God; in fact, a lot of the bad we go through comes from our enemy Satan, but we assume it's God and tend to blame him. If you are a follower in Christ, then you know that what the enemy means for bad, God makes for our good.

This leads me into Jesus our Redeemer and what it is he did for us. You see, God already knew that we would succumb to sin and that an animal sacrifice like in the Old Testament were not going to be enough to save us to make us pure enough to be in his presence. He knew it would require a sacrifice of the highest holiness, a pureness, a sacrifice of himself. So he sent his only begotten son for those who believe shall not perish but have everlasting life (John 3:16). Jesus was the ultimate sacrifice; he paid the full price with his blood for you and me and offered us a place at his table if we accepted his invitation.

THE SPIRIT OF ANGER

I've been saying a lot about the spirits that accompany drug use, and now I would like to talk about something that goes hand and hand with addiction, which is the spirit of anger. As an addict, we are so angry about what we have become; oftentimes, we are our biggest critic. Even though we hate ourselves, we portray that hate outwardly to the world. A lot of us feel as though it was all our circumstances that made us this way, and because of that, it's everyone's else's fault but ours that we have all this anger. In my struggle getting clean, this was one of the hardest obstacles for me to overcome because anger was such a big trigger in my drug use; it was one of my go-to tools when I needed to get him. I would use it as a crutch. I'm sure many of you have experience in this where you start a fight with your partners so you can go get high and have an excuse the next day to justify your actions. I know because I did this quite often.

If you haven't figured this out yet, anger is a big part of using it as a way of escaping from those that hurt us. If we get angry and blame it on someone or something that hurt us. We have just justified why we need to take that drug or that drink because we need it to control our anger, right? Well, not always the case; we think we are managing our anger when we are only covering our anger for a moment. It will come to the surface so much more profane, when we are under the influence. Because now, that angry spirit has taken our body completely hostage and we have become a puppet to their bidding. We end up hurting ourselves, but what's more is we end up hurting those we love most. Remember, these spirits are evil, and this is exactly what they want: they want you to destroy your life and the lives of others. That is their goal: to kill, steal, and destroy you and your family and friends. They are very well rehearsed in tearing up marriages and families and taking lives through suicide.

Eventually, we become such angry people that no one wants to be around us, including ourselves. The anger eats us inside and leaves us feeling empty and sad without hope or support from our loved ones because of the destruction we bring to their lives.

Anger can become sinful when it is motivated by pride (James 1:20), when it is unproductive and thus distorts God's purposes (1 Corinthians 10:31), or when anger is allowed to linger (Ephesians 4:26–27). One obvious sign that anger has turned to sin is when, instead of attacking the problem at hand, we attack the wrongdoer (Ephesians 4:15–19). Jesus says we are to speak the truth in love and use our words to build others up, not allow rotten or destructive words to pour from our lips. Unfortunately, this poisonous speech is a common characteristic of fallen man (Romans 3:14–15). Anger becomes sin when it is allowed to boil over without restraint, resulting in a scenario in which hurt is multiplied (Proverbs 29:11), leaving devastation in its wake. Often, the consequences of out-of-control anger are irreparable. Anger also becomes sin when the angry one refuses to be pacified, holds a grudge, or keeps it all inside (Ephesians 4:26–27). This can cause depression and irritability over little things, which are often unrelated to the underlying problem.

We can handle anger biblically by recognizing and admitting our prideful anger and/or our wrong handling of anger as sin (Proverbs 28:13). This confession should be both to God and to those who have been hurt by our anger. We should not minimize the sin by excusing it or blame-shifting.

We can handle anger biblically by seeing God in the trial as the judge. This is especially important when people have done something to offend us; we must give it to God and let him take justice for their wrong actions against us. James 1:2–4, Romans 8:28–29, and Genesis 50:20 all point to the fact that God is sovereign over every circumstance and person that crosses our path. Nothing happens to us that He does not cause or allow. Though God does allow bad things to happen, He is always faithful to redeem them for the good of His people. God is good (Psalms 145:8, 9, 17). Reflecting on this truth until it moves from our heads to our hearts will alter how we react to those who hurt us.

We can handle anger biblically by making room for God's wrath. This is especially important in cases of, when "evil" men abuse "innocent" people. Genesis 50:19 and Romans 12:19 both tell us to not play God.

We can handle anger biblically by returning good for evil (Genesis 50:21; Romans 12:21). This is key to converting our anger into love. As our actions flow from our hearts, so also our hearts can be altered by our actions (Mathew 5:43–48). That is, we can change our feelings toward another by changing how we choose to act toward that person.

We must act to solve our part of the problem (Romans 12:18). We cannot control how others act or respond, but we can make the changes that need to be made on our part. Overcoming a temper is not accomplished overnight. But through prayer, Bible study, and reliance upon God's Holy Spirit, ungodly anger can be overcome. We may have allowed anger to become entrenched in our lives by habitual practice, but we can also practice responding correctly until that, too, becomes a habit and God is glorified in our response.

THE SPIRIT OF DEPRESSION

Depression can overtake someone to the point that life is hopeless; getting clean is not an option for many. I've heard many women tell me they would rather stay high than to get clean and face what horrible things they have done in their addiction. Many women dreamt of the fairy tale growing up. A husband that will love them, a beautiful house with a white picket fence, and children. When they have taken wrong turns in life and they have no children because they have been taken by the system because of drugs and/or alcohol, they have no husband because they have no self-respect for their bodies. They die inside, and hopelessness and depression take over completely; they have nothing to live for except that next high. What these women haven't found is Jesus. Once Jesus is found in them, then they will understand that their hopelessness was all a lie from Satan. He wants you to believe there is no hope. But there's a God that tells us he will restore us if we turn over our lives to him.

Depression can take on many faces; it can come from generational curses from soul wounds. This spiritual sickness, these demons, can often overcome us taking our thoughts captive to the point that we become suicidal. It can also take us down the road of destruction, for ourselves and others. Depression will manifest into other demonic influences such as anger, bitterness, unforgiveness. It will lie to you, telling you how unworthy of love you are, how no one could love you because of your self-appearance.

Repent therefore, and turn again, that your sins may be blotted out, that times of refreshing may come from the presence of the Lord, and that he may send the Christ appointed for you, Jesus, whom heaven must receive until the time for restoring all the things about which God spoke by the mouth of his holy prophets long ago. (Acts 3:19–21)

To appoint unto them that mourn in Zion, to give unto them beauty for ashes, the oil for joy for morning they might be called trees of righteousness, the planting of the Lord he might be glorified. (Isaiah 61:3)

Our heart can be downcast when depression rears its ugly head. This spirit can bring heaviness over us; it will rob our hope. It brings a heavy oppressed feeling and steals our faith. The spirit of depression will try to overcome us like a dark heaviness. It can come all at once like a sickness. It causes us to isolate, it steals our love, makes us feel alone, and steals our relationship with God. So in all things related to depression, put on the garment of praise to God and sing out loud with all your heart and soul and your depression will flee. For evil cannot stand or reside in the praising and glorifying of God.

Depression can come from a number of traumas that have occurred in our lives: death, relationships, self-worth, pain incurred from a loved one, and loneliness, the feeling of being all alone.

Proverbs 12:25 mentions depression directly, "Anxiety in the heart of man causes depression, but a good word makes it glad."

That's a good place to begin. In this little couplet, God, via the wisdom of Solomon, provides both a diagnosis and prescription that can help people grow beyond depression. A heart full of anxiety is the culprit. Jesus said:

Come to Me, all you who are weary and burdened, and I will give you rest. Take My yoke upon you, and learn from Me, because I am gentle and humble in heart, and you will find rest for your souls. For My yoke is easy, and My burden is light. (Mathew 11:28–30)

For some, depression comes with confusion and agitation; it is usually caused by emotional buildup and usually brings fear. Fear does not come from God.

For God has not given us a spirit of fear but of Power, Love and of a sound mind. (2 Tim 1:7)

To defeat this oppression of depression, we need to be thankful to Jesus Christ that we are saved. Sing. Rejoice! Thank him for your health. Thank him and thank him again and again and again for all he does and is.

The more we thank him, the less we will be in a selfish pit or murmuring. We must kill all self-pity if we want to escape.

In everything give thanks for this is the will of God in Christ Jesus concerning you. (1 Thessalonians 5:18)

As Christians, we have a hard time doing this, but this is the Bible's way God's way, of getting free from depression, not like man's way of taking a pill! Get out of the darkness, and let the sunshine on our lives again!

Put on the garment of praise.

Pray this prayer when heaviness comes on:

Thank you, Father, I have the authority from the finished work of your son. I rebuke this spirit of heaviness. I command it to leave me in the Name of Jesus. I bind the spirit and command it to leave me. I resist the heaviness and depression, and because I am submitted to God, it must and will flee (James 4:7).

MORE STRATEGIES FOR DEALING WITH DEPRESSION

Describe the experience. Describe your experience of depression in vivid detail. People are different, so depression comes in many shapes and sizes.

Identify the causes. Depression often is not just something we have; it is something we do. Examine your own hearts with this question: If your depression could speak, what would it say? What does it say about you? To others? To God? Depression is an active experience and can result from many sources other than the physiological: guilt due to unconfessed sin, false guilt, misplaced shame, ungodly fears, suppressed bitterness or hatred, hopeless grieving, and unbiblical expectations.

Read and observe Scripture. Ask people with whom you work to study Psalms 42–43. How does the psalmist address God? What does he preach to himself?

Act on the truth. Those who seek help first must accept the challenge of faithful obedience; even though they do not feel like it and are skeptical that anything will make a difference, it's important to have faith. Also, to progress out of the pit is step by step, bit by bit. Small, practical, consistent faith-based change occurs in the details.

Look at your lifestyle. Evaluate and listen to recommendations for lifestyle problems, such as overworking, lack of exercise, sleep difficulties, procrastination, unresolved stressors, absence of spiritual disciplines.

Resolve conflicts. Deal with troubled relationships, past or present.

Get to work. Do loving tasks performed for the benefit of others. Helping others can provide a new perspective on life.

This is where God's people can help those of us with depression; we can find them at churches or at Bible studies. We can also find help through local organizations that help the broken, like shelters or soup kitchens where volunteering time is very rewarding and takes away from the troubles of our own lives.

WE HAVE HOPE IN GOD AND JOY IN SALVATION

God encourages us to "call upon him in the day of trouble; I will deliver you" (Psalm 50:15).

Hopelessness is a hallmark of depression. The grace of God in Jesus Christ is the sum of all hope.

> God wanted to make known among the Gentiles the glorious wealth of this mystery, which is Christ in you, the hope of glory. (Colossians 1:27)

> Paul, a man who had more than his share of tribulation and suffering, proclaimed, "We have placed our hope in Him that He will deliver us again." (2 Corinthians 1:10)

We live in a fallen world, one in which good things may come to an end. The tragic dimension of life will be present until the kingdom of God comes fully in Jesus's return. The joy of salvation comes from realizing, again and again, that our sins have been forgiven and that we will live forever with the eternally happy God, who desires that we share in His joy. We should never "get over" the gospel.

We should show active love for God and others.

Love for God and others is essential because we all at some time or another find ourselves sucked into a vortex of morbid self-involvement, which keeps us from following the heavenly prescription given by the Great Physician, the medicine that many need above all else.

"Teacher, who command in the law is the greatest?" He said to him, "Love the Lord your God
with all your heart, with all your soul, and with
all your mind. This is the greatest and most
important command. The second is like it: Love
your neighbor as yourself. All the Law and the
Prophets depend on these two commands."
(Matthew 22:36–40)

When we begin to love God with all our heart, soul, mind, and
strength and demonstrate love to others, we find true hope in God's
active love.

Satan often uses others that you love most to hurt you.

Often, sexual immorality like adultery will tear a marriage apart.
Adultery can be emotional or physical for a woman. Emotional adultery wreaks havoc on a woman's heart. It is more personal for her
because instead of it being a physical action of a one-night stand, it
is ongoing pillow talk that all women long for from their husbands.
For a man, physical adultery wreaks havoc on his reputation; it takes
away his respect that the wife is to honor her husband with. Looking
at other men and women naked (pornography) is the same as having
an affair; it is lust of the eyes, and in Mathew 5:27, Jesus warns that
if a man looks at woman with wrong intention, lust, he has already
committed adultery in his heart which is a sin. For this will also
doom a marriage in time, the husband and/or wife will build resentment and bitterness toward the other, leading to divorce.

Satan doesn't only use sexual immorality to destroy marriages;
he is very cunning in using many sins such as unforgiveness, lies,
sorcery (drug use), anger, violence. All of these or the majority will be
used against you to destroy your relationship and your marriage, and
without Jesus in the middle of our marriage, we are doomed. Jesus
is the way, and we must allow him to take over our lives completely.
Run to him, fall at your knees, and praise him, pray for those that
come against you and allow God to be your defender. One thing
that we must understand if we want our prayers to be heard and to
be children of God. We must live under the house rules of God our

Father and give up the life of this world and obey God in everything we do that means giving up all sin. This means turning our lives completely around from the shows we watch to the music we listen to the people we surround ourselves with to giving ourselves completely to God and obeying his word.

A Prideful Spirit

Spirit of pride can definitely trip you up in many ways. Many times, we don't even realize we are being prideful or causing people to feel hurt or, worse, to feel unwelcome. So let's learn about the subject of pride in the Bible and see what it says about having a haughty spirit.

> Whoever loves a quarrel loves sin; whoever builds
> a high gate invites destruction. (Proverbs 17:19)

Pride is a dangerous master. All of us have seen great leaders, athletes, movie stars, and many friends fall on their faces because they allowed their pride to take control of their spirits.

> He also told this parable to some who trusted in themselves that they were righteous, and treated others with contempt: "Two men went up into the temple to pray, one a Pharisee and the other a tax collector. The Pharisee, standing by himself, prayed thus: 'God, I thank you that I am not like other men, extortioners, unjust, adulterers, or even like this tax collector. I fast twice a week; I give tithes of all that I get.' But the tax collector, standing far off, would not even lift up his eyes to heaven, but beat his breast, saying, 'God, be merciful to me, a sinner!'" (Luke 18:9–14)

For the sin of their mouths, the words of their
lips, let them be trapped in their pride. For the
cursing and lies that they utter. (Psalm 59:12)

Pride is such a huge part of our being; it encompasses our whole
lives, our relationships, our work, our family. It was the sin that had
Lucifer casted out of heaven. He thought he was better than God
and could do a better job; he wanted the power of God to be his. Of
course, we have only one Father, one Lord in heaven that is the alpha
and the omega. This is what Satan didn't realize: God is all powerful;
he is his creator and his under.

Pride is one of the biggest tools that Satan uses to tear people
apart. Men especially have a sense to prove themselves to think that
they can be the hero to their wives, and when they fall short, it turns
to resentment. Problem is that we have Satan spiritually attacking
us in our marriages and relationships. Men or women cannot solve
these problems without the help of God.

Women have a sense of pride in showing off their physical bodies to others, because of the stigma of self-worth in our society. When
they don't meet the expectations of what they are taught, what the
world has set its standards on beauty physically they fall into self-
pity and pride. You see, it's a catch-22 when you are of the world.
But if you choose to follow God, he is the only one that matters,
and pleasing him will be your first and foremost concern. Outward
appearance becomes not so important as inward appearance.

Many times, while dealing with my own addictions, I was told
that we keep our problems to ourselves because it brings shame upon
the family. This is a complete lie from Satan, of course he's going
to put these thoughts of guilt and shaming on us. He doesn't want
anyone to be spiritually saved and to be happy. So we keep all this
anger and resentment bitterness bottled up so that we don't look like
we have problems for others. This is such a crucial part of giving over
our lives to God; we must humble ourselves to God and God's people
in order to begin healing; if we pretend that everything is all right,
we will see our lives fall to complete destruction for depending on
own strength. We are not strong enough; have you figured that out

yet? We need Jesus. He is the only way we will ever be able to have victory once we have Jesus in our lives. We then come from victory, not to victory.

"God opposes, resists, abhors, tears down, brings down, has scattered, is scornful to, reprimands, will punish, is angry at, every arrogant person, those who have a proud look, those whose pride wells up, arrogant scoffers. The prideful man will be brought low, humiliated, disgraced, doomed, destroyed, humbled, will not go unpunished, was deposed from his royal throne and his honor was removed" (Proverbs 3:34, 11:2, 16:5, 15:25, 29:23; Psalm 18:27, 101:5, 119:21; Isaiah 2:11,12, 10:12; 2 Chronicles 32:25; Daniels 5:20; Luke 1:51; James 4:6). This is a really serious thing.

We'll never conquer pride, but if we know what it looks like when it flares up, we can knock it back down before too much damage is done. If people can't recognize what the signs of cancer look like, then they'll never know they need help. I hope this list helps you understand what pride looks like as much as it's helped me.

DEFINITION OF PRIDE

Our self or ego is basically who we are as a person. It's not good or bad, it's just what makes us. Unhealthy pride happens when we do or say things for the purpose of people praising our self or for making our self feel good or putting our self ahead of someone else. Pride wants our self to be praised, get glory, be worshiped, and be highly talked about, even when we're not in the room. Unhealthy pride can give us an elevated view of our own self that is not accurate, but we truly start to believe it and act to reinforce what we've come to believe as true. And when someone questions or challenges the view of our self as not accurate, the fireworks begin.

Here are some more definitions of pride I found:

- Pride is being self-is
- Thinking excessively about self
- Pride's base is too much self-love

- Thinking the worth of our self is higher than it actually is
- Self-worship
- Preoccupation with our image or self
- Pride is narcissism (in love with our image or self)
- Pride is self-centered or ego-centric (everything revolves around us)
- Pride wants to keep the focus on self
- Self-ness

Satan disguises submission to himself under the ruse of personal autonomy. He never asks us to become his servants. Never once did the serpent say to Eve, "I want to be your Master." The shift in commitment is never from Christ to evil; it is always from Christ to self. And instead of his will, self-interest now rules and what I want reigns. And that is the essence of sin. (Dennis F. Kinlaw (1922–2017))

Instead of being motivated by SELF-is ambition or vanity, each of you should, in humility (THE OPPOSITE OF PRIDE OR SELFISH), be moved to treat one another as more important than your-SELF. Each should be concerned not only about your own interests, but about the interests of others as well. (Philippians 2:3–4)

Jesus said to him, "Love the Lord your God with all your heart, with all your soul and with all your mind. This is the first and greatest commandment. The second is like it: Love your neighbor as you love your SELF. All the law and the prophets depend on these two commandments." (Matthew 22:37–39)

Love is patient, love is kind, it is not envious. Love does not brag; it is not puffed up. It is not rude, it is not Self-serving, it is not easily angered or resentful. (All the negatives are symptoms of pride.) (1 Corinthians 13:4–5)

But be careful not to judge a person's heart because of their actions or words. You can't always tell. A friend of mine, who is a huge servant and genuinely humble, told me that when he serves others, he usually thinks, "I sure hope they feel cared for and loved." But now and then, he serves and says, "I bet they think I'm quite the servant. I bet they think I'm humble." Don't try to play God and judge the heart.

PRIDE OF SPIRITUALITY

- Try really hard to confirm the fact that they're spiritual.
- Asceticism: They reject money, pleasure, joy, fame, or possessions. (They mistakenly think God likes that.)
- Brag about how *not* materialistic they are.
- Excessively give away nice possessions or money that God gives them.
- Tell everyone, "I gave up a high-paying career to do this ministry."
- Make excuses for the physical blessings in their life.
- Look down their self-righteous noses at the wealthy or successful.

SUPER CHRISTIAN PRIDE

- Spiritualize every conversation.
- Speak with a different accent or voice about spiritual stuff.
- Think they're more spiritual or righteous than others around them.
- Feel morally superior.
- Despise and detest sinners.
- Insist on having certain roles in the church that they're disqualified or not qualified for, just to prove to people that they're spiritual.
- Talk a lot about their spiritual gift of apostle or prophet, but not about the less public ones.
- Talk about how much they pray.

- Look down on or badmouth Christians or other denominations who believe differently than they do about spiritual gifts.
- Talk about their fasting so that people know they're fasting. "When you fast, do not look sullen like the hypocrites, for they make their faces unattractive so that people will see them fasting. I tell you the truth, they have their reward" (Matthew 6:16).
- Prayer isn't from the heart. "Whenever you pray, do not be like the hypocrites, because they love to pray while standing in synagogues and on street corners so that people can see them. Truly I say to you, they have their reward" (Matthew 6:5).
- Rehearse or spruce up their public prayers using different words and phrases that they would never say when praying alone.
- Talk to the people when they say they are praying to God. Give mini sermonettes.
- Say "I'll pray for that" when they absolutely have no intention of praying for it. But it sounds spiritual for sure.
- False humility: Humility is seeing yourself and what you do the way it actually is. Pride is not seeing yourself or what you do the way it actually is.
- Don't accept compliments, but instead say, "Thank you but no. It was all God." (If it were all God, it would have been *way* better than you did it.)
- Say that they're lower and worse than everyone else.
- Tell you that they're humble, "In my humble opinion."

PRIDE OF KNOWLEDGE

- Try really hard to confirm the fact that they're smart.
- Unteachable.
- Get irritated if someone tries to teach them something.
- Know it all.
- Answer "I know, I know" or "Yeah, I already knew that."

- Too smart for a formal education or training. "But what could I learn?"
- Highly opinionated.
- Often interrupt people mid-sentence: "I don't mean to interrupt, but…"
- Finish other people's sentences: "I know what you're going to say. You were going to say…"
- Often try to prove people wrong.
- If questioned, they say, "Don't you think I know what I'm doing?"
- Don't listen to the ideas or wisdom of those they lead.
- Use big words and then explain them to you.
- Despise and detest people of other political beliefs.
- Defensive when corrected or criticized. If you ever get defensive in marriage, then you have pride, and it has to be dealt with. We think the best defense is a great offense when our pride is hurt. "With pride comes only contention" (Proverbs 13:10).
- Attack back when questioned or confronted about a mistake or wrong.
- Struggle admitting a wrong.
- Defend their kids and attack anyone who addresses their kid's wrong behavior (because they think it reflects bad on them).
- Refuse to or are slow to say, "I was wrong. Will you forgive me?"
- Blame everyone else but themselves.
- Set up excuses in advance so it isn't their fault.
- Lie or make up excuses when corrected or criticized.
- Say things like, "Everybody makes mistakes. Heck, you make mistakes too."
- Argumentative, just have to be right.
- Don't discuss differences to learn, just to show off how much they know.
- "Told you so." Remind you about when they were right and you were wrong.

- Get the last word.
- Argue strange, hard to defend beliefs or doctrines to impress with their intellect.
- Critical: highlight other's flaws to make their self feel better.
- Quick to correct or criticize spouses, kids, pastors, and other leaders.
- Criticize with no intention of building up or improving the situation.
- Harsh teasing to tear down.
- Negative and complain a lot.
- Don't show much mercy.
- Mean spirited.

PRIDE OF POWER

- Try really hard to confirm the fact that they're capable. "But once he became powerful, his pride destroyed him. He disobeyed the Lord his God" (2 Chronicles 26:16).
- Controlling: being obeyed gives their self a nice feeling, sense of power.
- Excessively taking care of and shielding their older children.
- Pay the consequences for their kid's irresponsibility.
- Manipulate to keep their adult children close.
- Try to control or sway their adult children's marriages.
- Use women and keep them hanging on.
- Throw their wedding ring, threaten to boycott events, scream, threaten divorce, withhold affection, or hit.
- Legalistic: Control through excessive rules; their self feels really nice when they are obeyed.
- Don't want kids to rebel mostly so that the parent's self or image isn't tarnished.
- Must have the appearance of spirituality in strict dress codes and grooming.
- King James Version is the only version you can read (huge red flag).
- Hold to a few chosen Old Testament laws.

- Won't submit: It makes their self falsely feel inferior if they have a positional leader, though it has nothing to do with wisdom, knowledge, or ability.
- Want the autonomy to decide how to live their life, so won't submit or surrender to God. "God opposes the proud, but he gives grace to the humble. So, submit to God. But resist the devil and he will flee from you. Draw near to God and he will draw near to you" (James 4:5–8).
- Hate being told to do anything.
- Will submit in the little things, but not in the big things.
- Church members won't submit to church leaders.
- Wives won't submit to husbands.
- Children won't submit to parents.
- Employees won't submit to employers.
- Self-reliant: Don't want or think they need guidance, help, or wisdom from God or man. "When they were fed, they became satisfied; when they were satisfied, they became proud; as a result, they forgot me!" (Hosea 13:6).

PRIDE OF INDEPENDENCE

- Fear or worry a lot because they depend on their own abilities.
- Hate to rely on others.
- Think their abilities are superior to others.
- Don't let others make decisions.
- Are bothered when a decision is made without them.
- Don't see much need for prayer.
- Willing to help, but not be helped.
- Willing to financially support, but can't ask for support.
- Rarely say the words "Thank you" to God or man. "But Hezekiah was ungrateful; he had a proud attitude, provoking God to be angry at him" (2 Chronicles 32:25).
- Excessive need for credit, praise, or admiration.
- Hungry to be made mention of for accomplishments, service, or selflessness.

- Lie about events or accomplishments, way beyond embellishing a story to make it fun.
- Lie to take credit for things they didn't do.
- Don't give compliments or credit to whom it is due.
- Hate sharing the spotlight.
- Shoot down or don't share other people's good ideas.
- Importance: They feel that the value of their self grows with accomplishments, status, wealth, or success. "By your great skill in trade you have increased your wealth, and your heart is proud because of your wealth" (Ezekiel 28:5).
- People who exploit others to get rich. Health and wealth televangelists, those who prey on the elderly's money etc.
- Think their worth to God is based on their sacrifices of time, family, or money.
- Think that everybody needs their help.
- Workaholic: believes work gives their self more worth.
- Believe that the value of their self is based on performance.
- Obsessed with praise for their discipline, schedule, productivity, or busyness.
- Love the feeling of their self being praised and built up more than they care about the self of their kids who don't believe their self is worth much anymore.
- Work long hours, doing work of two to three people.
- Serve or work so much that it hurts their family relationships.
- Volunteers for everything.
- Hungry to be depended on.
- Can't say no.
- People pleaser.
- Can't set boundaries.
- Don't delegate much.
- Grandiosity: Think they are superior to the common man, in their essence, to the point that some even believe they are godlike.
- Condescending and disdainful attitude toward people because of their tastes being inferior to theirs in food, restaurants, sports, movies, and other likes and dislikes.

- Look down their noses, demeans, belittles, intimidates, bullies others whose likes or dislikes differ from their own superior ones.
- Have an unrealistic sense of, and sustained view of, their own self as better than other people.
- Have a strong sense of personal uniqueness or coolness.
- Believe that few people have anything in common with their self.
- Believe that their self can only be understood by very few and special people.
- Boastful and arrogant. "Proud men will be brought low, arrogant men will be humiliated" (Isaiah 2:11).
- Overly materialistic, hoping people will think more highly of their self.
- Skillfully brag about their successful ministry, in a humble-sounding way.
- Hint around at their success.
- Claim that they're a genius or one of the best ever or one of the best on their team.
- Talk a lot about their importance, status, accomplishments, possessions, education, title, position, credentials, or financial status.
- Name drop the high-status people they associate with.
- Surround themselves with good-looking or successful people.
- Think certain tasks would lower their image or value of their self.
- Think they're above certain tasks.
- Feel entitled to high treatment.
- Feel superior to or are prejudiced toward less wealthy, refined, educated, or less successful people or those from a different country or culture.
- Inconvenience others: the world revolves around their self. Self-centered, ego-centric, self-absorbed.
- Feel powerful when people have to wait on them. I often wonder if people who drive slow in the fast lane and won't let people pass are just jerks or just ignorant.

- Regularly make everyone wait on them to get to the meeting so they can start.
- Inconsiderate. Don't consider other people's time.
- Not interested in other people.
- Rarely ask questions of others because they're more interested in their self than in the self of others.
- Dominate conversations talking about their self, thinking, or how much they know so that we're impressed with their self.
- Rarely compliment people.
- Wait to be served instead of serving.
- Neglect others.
- Not generous.
- Abandon their family to pursue their own self feeling good.
- Low self-esteem or self-worth: Humility is seeing your own self the way it actually is. Pride is not seeing your own self the way it actually is.
- Constantly thinking of their self and what others think about it.
- Feel inferior.
- Think they're not worthy of a good spouse or job.
- Constantly dating abusive people.

SELF-LOATHING

- Believe that people don't like them.
- Avoid successful or attractive people.
- Put their self down so that others affirm and build them up.
- Often say that they're ugly.
- Make excuses for their nationality: "But I'm of European descent."
- Self-conscious for lack of education, beauty, social, or economic status.
- Don't share their shortcomings or needs.
- Depression: There are a lot of legitimate medical and traumatic reasons for depression. Focus on self and believing

what's not true about their self is a very common one. Pride is a major cause of depression for hundreds of millions of people (much more about why this is here, on the second list).

- Shyness: this isn't about introvert or extrovert.
- Overly concerned with others' opinions of their self.

SOCIAL ISOLATION PRIDE

- Are afraid of not being liked.
- Are afraid of being criticized.
- Are afraid of being rejected again.
- Are afraid of embarrassing themselves.

HIGHLY SENSITIVE PRIDE

- Read into innocent remarks as demeaning, threatening, or critical.
- Can't laugh at themselves when they do something funny.
- Can't accept good-natured teasing.
- Have a hard time forgiving.
- Are offended when their idea, ability, or motive is questioned.
- Quick to be angry.
- Envious: think that when others have things they don't, it makes their self look bad. "For where there is jealousy and Selfishness, there is disorder and every evil practice" (James 3:16–17).
- Constantly compare themselves to others.
- Bothered when someone equal to them has success.
- Wants other people's status symbols to make their self look better.
- Sabotage those close to them so good things or success won't happen.
- Believe other people are envious of them.

PRIDE OF APPEARANCE

- Try really hard to impress people with their looks or physique. Synonyms: narcissistic, self-love, conceited, self-glorification, egotistic, self-worship. "Your heart was proud because of your beauty; you corrupted your wisdom on account of your splendor" (Ezekiel 28:17). Though it is important that we do the best with the hand we were dealt, especially for our spouse.
- Feel their appearance gives their self more worth.
- Think their beauty makes their self superior to others.
- Flaunt their figure/physique so others will praise them.
- Spend excessive time on hair, clothing, weight, body shape to impress.
- Anorexia or bulimia.
- Work hard to avoid the appearance of aging.
- Often post photos or videos of themselves exercising.
- Spend excessive time for their self to look good while neglecting family.

I didn't write these, I researched pride. Don't shoot the messenger. I'm just reporting the facts. These signs of pride are what I found and copied down and then consolidated here for your reading pleasure. Most were on several of the lists.

If you only saw yourself in a couple of places on this list, then you just have a little bit of cancer. You need to be desperate for treatment. Everyone is infected with pride. Don't be okay with it. This is serious.

> But then Hezekiah and the residents of Jerusalem humbled themselves and abandoned their pride, and the Lord was not angry with them for the rest of Hezekiah's reign. (2 Chronicles 32:26)

> If people who are called by my name humble themselves and pray and seek my face and turn

from their wicked ways, then I will hear from heaven and will forgive their sin and heal their land. Now my eyes will be open and my ears attentive to the prayer that is made in this place. (2 Chronicles 7:14–15)

Humble yourselves before the Lord and he will exalt you. (James 4:5)

But one who is humble, has a lowly spirit, will gain honor, wisdom, be exalted, shown favor, be listened to, receive grace" (free gifts that we don't deserve or earn. Unmerited favor.) (Proverbs 3:34, 29:23, 11:2; James 4:5, 10; 2 Chronicles 7:14)

A COMPLAINING SPIRIT

We have all complained at one point or another especially when things get difficult. We blame God for not taking us out of the situation we are in and begin to question God, "Why, Lord, why me, why does this happen to me?" sound familiar. We need to repent from blaming God and begin to thank him for what he has given us, as Job did. For if we resist the devil, he shall flee. Paul is an example to us all in Acts 16. Paul was thrown into prison; he could have complained and asked God, "Why God, why?" Instead, he gave God thanks. When we give God thanks in bad situations, it makes demons mad. The demons want you to be miserable, so when you give God thanks and praise, they flee. Therefore, resist the enemy and begin restoring your faith by giving thanks and praise. Ask God to restore you; find the courage in Christ to persevere until the enemy flees.

Paul and Silas with their backs bloody in a filthy prison did not get into the "poor me" self-pity attitude; they gave thanks. Demons like it when Christians complain; they try to manipulate us into blaming God. Which is a very bad thing to do. This will bring darkness into your life. Repent when self-pity starts to show in you.

In everything give thanks. (1 Thessalonians 5:18)

Get to the place that you are giving thanks all the time, not just in church, but on your worst days, when things are going wrong. Remember, everyone goes through struggles; if we claim to be children of God, we will give thanks even in our darkest hour.

ARE YOU READY TO CLAIM VICTORY IN JESUS CHRIST?

If you are, then it is time "to put off your old self which belongs to your old manner of life and is corrupt through deceitful desires and be renewed in the spirit of your minds, and put on the new self, created after the likeness of God in true righteousness and holiness" (Ephesians 4:22–24).

It is time my friends to stop being blind take off your blindfold, remove your ear plugs, see and hear what is on the horizon. For if you feel like Jesus is calling to you, it is time to take your place among his army and become the warrior that he has called you to be. We are his watchmen! We sound the alarm to others and let them know the enemy is at the door! For the time has come, Jesus is coming. Are you ready for that day when your king comes with his army to take back this world and his children?

For the enemy has already taken so much from you, it's time to rise up and fight back, take back what is rightfully yours, salvation through Jesus!

Break free from your chains of bondage; you can do all things through Jesus Christ. For God gave us a spirit of love, power, and self-discipline; just call upon him to come into your life, surrender yourself to him. If you are struggling with addiction, surrender today to Jesus, give your life to him today. Find a faith-based treatment center. If you take the first step and surrender, God will carry you the rest of the way.

Say this prayer if you are ready to give your life to Jesus:

Thank you, Jesus, for hearing from me today. Satan, you will not rule my life anymore. I freely give my life, my soul, and my spirit to my Lord and Savior Jesus Christ. Jesus, I ask that you come into my heart; break these chains of bondage to sin. Father, forgive me for all I have done to you and others, in the name of your son, Jesus. I take claim to what Jesus Christ did for me on that cross when he died for my sins and rose after the third day to be seated at the right hand of my Father God. I forgive those that sinned against me and let go of the resentment, bitterness, anger, jealousy I have held against others in my heart for so long. I ask for complete healing in my life, for restoration from all the enemy has taken from me. I call upon the Holy Spirit to lead me on the path to righteousness and give me a heart to serve you others. Armor me up, Father, that I may fight against the evil that comes to destroy me and my family. Help me to have the courage to stand up for righteousness and tell my testimony of your goodness and mercy. Be a light under my feet that I may go out and spread your word as your faithful disciple. Amen!

THE BATTLE BEGINS

The first thing in any battle is to know your opponent's weaknesses in order to use this and attack. The enemy hates to hear praise to God, so praise God and give him thanks throughout the day and the enemy will flee.

Once you have accepted Jesus Christ as our Lord and Savior of your life and turned your life around, the battle begins. The enemy has lost his grip on you, the chains of bondage are broken, your eyes are becoming open to the enemies' deceptions (lies) and manipulations. Temptation will flood into your life; it will be all around you, because Satan wants his puppet back. Remember that Jesus is stronger though. Satan has many tricks up his sleeve, so you must stay in your word. Feed your spirit constantly with the word of God that it may become strong and the words of God become written on your heart. Walk in righteousness; stay away from people that live in sin. Change your way of life; by this, you will have to do a complete turnaround from the music you listen to, to the movies you watch. We cannot be under the influence of this world any longer for Satan has corrupted it. The world will be against you and its ideals, but you must stay strong to the way of God or it will sneak its way back into your life. Because we are only human, there will be times when we fall. Jesus was crucified on the cross for such a time. That we may ask to be forgiven and then continue walking in righteousness.

I knew right after I gave my life and became a follower of Christ that my life I lived previously was all a lie, everything in it. The devil had deceived me, and I lived in complete darkness. I was under a demonic influence that had me thinking I couldn't survive without drugs. I needed them to function. That my body just wasn't able to recover and I would never be able to function as a mom or a wife again. I was under a spell, only to believe that nothing or no one could help me except for the drugs. It was the only thing that made me feel better. I was in complete darkness, lost in sin. I would do anything for the drug, to escape, to get that relief from the voices telling me what a horrible mother, daughter, person I was, reminding me of the destruction and pain I caused to myself and others.

Once I found Jesus and found a better way of living his way, my health came back, and my pain subsided. It was then I realized the drugs were keeping my body sick. I was able to do things that I couldn't do in years. This really made me mad to know that I had been deceived for so many years by Satan. I found this anger in me, but it was a righteous anger, an anger that hated sin. Satan was not going to win any longer. I was angry that he stole so much time from me that I was not going to give him another second! I called to my Father God asking for complete restoration of my family and life and I would walk in his ways forever.

Now that I gave my life, I was under attack by Satan. He was nowhere near letting go of me. But I knew I was not going to give him another minute of my life to steal. I began seeking God with all my heart, and as I did this, I got further and further away from sin. Don't get me wrong, I'm not saying I'm a saint, but God transforms us to his likeness when we seek him. So that when we do sin, we get conviction, and we get punished for our sin.

Even though the trials would come, I knew that it was just another test, another deception, for what the devil means for bad, God always makes for our good. I finally understood that God was with me and is with me through all the struggles, failures, pain, and sorrow I encounter and works it out for my good in his time.

My battle began the minute I turned over my life to Christ, and I knew it was going to be a fight. I ended up doing two years in prison. This was where my training ground began. God removed every influence in my life, and I became completely dependent on him. I was still able to talk with my family and receive visits, but other than that, it was me and the Lord, with Satan in the background, always trying to trip me up.

My time in prison opened my eyes and ears to God. I was humiliated and learned a lot of self-discipline especially when you are trying to live a godly life in a prison. God sent women into my life that would be an inspiration to me; even though they fell short at times as we all do, they loved Jesus with all their heart. I met my pastor and his wife who were amazing God-fearing people that had a huge heart for others and always served the Lord. They also were inspirations in my walk with God; in fact, the teachings I learned from my pastor's wife were invaluable. She showed me that we carry generational curses and soul wounds. These things are important aspects of learning as we walk with the Father for healing and cleansing.

The more I sought after God, the more I saw and learned about his greatness; in Isaiah 40, it gives an awesome description of who the Father is. Our world is a mere speck of dust. He is the creator of the universe, the Alpha and the Omega; his thinking is so much greater than ours that there is no comparison. We could never know the outcome of our decisions, but God does.

While in our pods, which consisted of about forty women, we were all lined up like sardines on bunk beds. We had a four-foot space between the beds, and all our belongings resided under our beds in containers. One weekend, I had been talking with one of my neighbors on the bed next to me when her neighbor rudely kept interrupting us about her views on the Bible. It agitated me so much, I finally told her to shut up and mind her own business. She got up and I got up, and the yelling match began. I'm in her face and she's in mine. We screamed out vulgarities to one another, saying the meanest things, knowing each other's dark secrets from meetings (RDAP) and using them against one another. I was able to walk out the door; something pulled me to the church, and I paced on the steps of our church and complained to God about her for hours. One of my friends from the church happened to be walking by and asked to pray with me. I hesitantly said okay. Then after I sat there for a while and God just kept putting it on my heart that I needed to apologize. This was crazy. I thought how could I apologize to her. She owed me the apology. I expressed to the Father, "You don't understand, Dad, I'm going to look like a fool, no one will respect me again. I'll be laughed at and looked upon as weak, and everyone will take advantage of me."

But the Father continued to tell me to apologize to her. I was upset by this response. Walking back to the pod, I argued with the Father, kicking rocks on the way, saying how unfair this was. One of the guards stopped to ask me if I was okay. I think he believed I had lost my mind because I was talking to myself or at least that's what he thought. When I told him I was talking to God, he looked at me with concern and silently walked away. When I finally got up the courage to do this, I walked in feeling like this is it, I'm going to be humiliated. I walked over to her with my head down and asked her to forgive me. I apologized sincerely for the things I said to her, and for a split moment, I thought that she would apologize back, but instead, her response was "You should be ashamed of yourself for talking like that to me, you shouldn't even work at a church, much less call yourself a child of God."

I took the scolding, biting my tongue, and keeping my head down. I just nodded and walked away. Something happened though. The women started coming up to me and telling me how I inspired them, and they said, "I can't believe she said that to you after you tried to apologize."

They started to look at me in a new way with greater respect. They told me that they knew I was changed by Jesus because they could see the forgiveness in me; they could see Jesus in me! To this day, I know that God was showing me humility and forgiveness and how to turn the other cheek. What I thought was going to be my end in the prison was actually my growth in Jesus.

For two years, I walked with the Father in that prison and learned many lessons in the face of adversity. I walked with God and talked with God every chance I got. I received my ordination while serving my sentence and learned that I was the happiest when I was telling of the goodness of our Savior Jesus Christ on that podium. I found what I wanted to do for the rest of my life, and that was to teach the words of God, talk about the Father and what he has done for me and what he can do for you.

Giving over our life to God means taking up our cross and getting ready for the battle that you have been asleep through. God will open your eyes and show you things, great and mighty things that you did not know of. Once your spiritual eyes are opened, you see the demons; you are able to pray and rage war against the enemy. This is a great honor for you know you're a soldier of the King of kings and Lord of lords, the Alpha and the Omega! You come from victory! For Jesus has already won the battle for us.

OUR ARMOR IN JESUS

Jesus, when he left to be with the Father, sent us a friend to guide; he sent us the Holy Spirit, but he also gave us his armor to protect us from Satan's attacks and he gave us weapons. Let me explain.

You may be familiar with the passage in Ephesians 6 where Paul calls us to put on the armor of God. Perhaps you have read through this passage before, but there is so much to be learned when we take a closer look and study it in-depth.

The armor of God represents the defense we must take in our spiritual lives. The Bible tells us that we are fighting a war against Satan, who seeks to destroy us. Therefore, we must take action and put on God's armor. As Christians, it is important for us to understand the severity of this battle. As it is often something we cannot physically see, it is easy to lose sight of the impact it can have. However, it can be very dangerous when we forget to equip ourselves with the armor of God; it allows the enemy to take control in our lives.

THE FIRST PIECE OF ARMOR IN EPHESIANS 6: THE BELT OF TRUTH

What is the belt of truth? Just what it says it is: the truth of who we are, the truth of who God is, the truth of the Word. In the beginning, the Word already existed; the Word was with God, and the Word was God. Through him, God made all things; not one thing in all creation was made without him. The Word was the source of life; it is the truth. What was made had life in union with the Word, and this life brought light to humanity. The light shines in the darkness, and the darkness has never put it out.

The truth will set you free from all the lies that Satan has deceived you with. The truth gives hope in hopeless situations. The truth is that God loves you; he knows every hair on your head. He knitted you to his perfection in the womb and knew you before you were ever conceived. God has always had a great purpose for your life, which is far greater than what we could ever imagine. But our choices have hindered our walk with the Father, and therefore, we have changed our purpose from what God wanted for us into conforming to our own selfish desires for riches and fame. He gives free will to everyone to choose who they shall serve, and it is never too late to begin your walk with God in truth and fulfill the purpose he meant for you. He gave you an instruction book on how to live, and it bears witness to the truth of all creation. Stop living in lies and fear of failure with God; there is only victory.

We must become woken to the truth, and that is by accepting God and his son Jesus Christ as our Savior and accepting the word of God. Once this awakening occurs, we can then understand who we are in God and what our purpose is.

The first piece of armor Paul discusses is the belt of truth. In Ephesians 6:14, he says, "Stand firm then, with the belt of truth buckled around your waist." Of all of the pieces of the armor of God, you may be wondering why Paul started with the belt. However, the belt plays a much more important role than we may think.

The belt is where Roman soldiers stored their weapon; without a belt, they could not carry a weapon! So why does Paul associate the belt of a soldier with truth? For Christians, God's Word is truth, and it serves as our foundation. In Roman soldier times, the belt covered and protected the soldier's genital area; it also held up the weight from the breastplate. In the same way, Paul chose to call the belt the belt of truth because it guards the truth of who we are!

How can we put on the armor of God in today's world? Well, in today's world, we see deception all around us; we see people changing what God made in his perfection. An example of the perversion of the truth: God made man and woman perfect in his eyes, yet society has perverted that by teaching that a man can be a woman and a woman a man when it is clearly stated in the Bible otherwise. But because of the sexual immorality all around us, it has become a normal part of life as in the days of Noah. If we feel we are attracted to the same sex all of a sudden, we question who we are, male or female, when clearly God has already made that distinction. Problem is people are looking for something to fulfill their life; they have an emptiness that is eating them up inside. People try to fill it with what they think is missing: money, cars, pornography, alcohol, drugs, the love of another. When in fact, that causes more pain.

We end up putting all our trust and hope in someone we believe loves us, which they might, but eventually, they will hurt us. It's human nature to sin, and no one is perfect except for our Father in heaven. That is why we put him first in our lives and make him number one. He will never hurt or abandon us. Sometimes, the opposite sex hurts us, and we believe that they all are the same. So in order to not get hurt again, we connect with the same sex and develop a relationship based on the assumption; they know what they desire love, feeling of safety and security and to be understood is. But the truth is God made us different for a purpose: he made woman to complete man. You see, we each bring differences to the relationship; for instance, a woman is a nurturer: she brings caring, understanding, and can calm her husband. She also is a great influencer to her husband. Whereas a man is more physical: he is hard-wired to work and provide and bring a respectable name to his family.

Not only was man and woman made for each other emotionally, but they were also made for each other physically to procreate and have Godly children in this was their blessing. Today, too many people don't see that children are your legacy; they are a blessing to the family. It is through them that your name lives on. But too many people search for riches in money and fame. We don't see that our riches are in our family. Knowing the truth can show you who you are in Christ and establish a relationship so the emptiness can be filled with God who wants to show you great and mighty things. He wants you to experience what he has in store for you, something greater than you can ever imagine.

God created man in His own image, in the image
of God He created him; male and female He created them. (Genesis 1:27)

Once we have our belt securely in place, we have a foundation
of truth we know right and wrong. How do we know this? Because
the Bible tells us so, God's Word is the truth, and if we are going
against this truth, we are going against God.

Do not let the enemy gain an inch of ground by deceiving you;
remember his mission is to destroy you.

Second Timothy 3:16 says, "All Scripture is God-breathed and
is useful for teaching, rebuking, correcting and training in righteousness." If our beliefs are not rooted in God's Word, we cannot expect
to fight battles for Christ.

BREASTPLATE OF RIGHTEOUSNESS

The second piece of the armor of God that Paul discusses in
Ephesians 6 is the breastplate of righteousness. To be righteous means
to obey God's commandments and live in a way that is honorable to
Him. Psalm 106:3 says, "How blessed are those who keep justice,
who practice righteousness at all times!"

What purpose does a breastplate serve?

The breastplate was a central part of the Roman soldier's
armor—it provided protection for the torso, which contains vital
organs like the heart, lungs, and so on. Without a breastplate, a soldier would be asking for death, as any attack could instantly become
fatal. With a sturdy breastplate, the very same attacks become inef-
fective and useless, as blows glance off the armor.

So at salvation, we are issued a breastplate. It is designed to
protect our heart and soul from deception. Our own righteous acts
are no match for Satan's attacks. We need supernatural power that is
given through Christ to us!

> We are all infected and impure with sin when we display our own righteous deeds; they are nothing but filthy rags. (Isaiah 64:6)

Faith and love also to protect our hearts. It's interesting to study how faith and love relate to righteousness. Faith works "through love" (Galatians 5:6), and Abraham's faith (which was shown by his doing what God said to do) was "accounted to him for righteousness" (Romans 4:3; Genesis 26:5). As the Jamieson, Fausset, and Brown commentary puts it: "'Faith,' as the motive within, and 'love,' exhibited in outward acts, constitute the perfection of righteousness" (note on 1 Thessalonians 5:8).

How do I wear the breastplate of righteousness? God issues the breastplate to you with Christ's name stamped on it as though he is saying, "Your righteousness is not good enough. Here, wear mine."

God instructs us to put on this armor. So how do we put it on? By seeking God and his righteousness. We make him and his place our dwelling place. We delight ourselves in his commands and desire his way to be our ways. When God reveals an area of change to us, we obey and allow him to work on us. Ephesians 6:13 says, "Therefore take up the whole armor of God, that you may be able to withstand in the evil day, and having done all, to stand."

So now we know what the breastplate of righteousness is. Paul gives us the command to "take up the whole armor of God"—the obvious question is "How?" An in-depth concordance study of all the scriptures concerning righteousness (there are 301 in the New King James Version!) reveals that servants of God in the Bible who had righteousness all had it because they followed God's way. Though it may seem a sweeping statement, it is through a continuing and dedicated adherence to both the letter and spirit of God's law that we can defend ourselves with His righteousness.

Once we have put on the breastplate of righteousness, we must be sure not to remove it. Ezekiel 33:13 shows that wearing righteousness is not a one-time event; rather, it requires a lifetime of action. One day, the war we're fighting will be over. And when it is, we are promised, "The work of righteousness will be peace, and the effect of righteousness, quietness and assurance forever" (Isaiah 32:17). By faithfully living God's way and staying clear of Satan's, we will find this peace, quietness, and assurance—forever. Do not allow your earthly concerns to crowd out time for an intimate relationship with God.

What does God say about righteousness?

> Riches do not profit on the day of wrath, but righteousness delivers from death. Without righteousness, we leave ourselves open to almost certain death. With righteousness—just as with a breastplate—the otherwise fatal attacks of our enemy are thwarted. (Proverbs 11:4)

> My tongue shall speak of Your word, for all Your commandments are righteousness. (Psalm 119:172)

> Whoever commits sin also commits lawlessness, and sin is lawlessness. (1 John 3:4)

> Awake to righteousness, and do not sin; for some do not have the knowledge of God. I speak this to your shame. (1 Corinthians 15:34)

To be righteous is to do what is right in God's eyes. God's commandments are righteousness. In contrast, lawlessness is sin, and sin is the opposite of righteousness. So to be righteous is to obey God's laws of love.

Unrighteousness, the separation from God:

> Behold, the Lord's hand is not shortened, that it cannot save; nor His ear heavy, that it cannot hear. But your iniquities have separated you from your God; and your sins have hidden His face from you, so that He will not hear. Iniquities

and sins are actions and thoughts that go against God's laws. (Isaiah 59:1–2)

Since they are in conflict with God's way of living and are harmful to ourselves and others, our perfect and just God will not associate with us if we go down the path of sin and evil. We cut ourselves off from God and His protection! It is interesting to note that in this same chapter, Isaiah mentions that God Himself puts on righteousness as a breastplate (Isaiah 59:17), which may be part of what inspired Paul to use this analogy.

Carelessness:

> Be sober, be watchful: your adversary the devil, as a roaring lion, walketh about, seeking whom he may devour: whom withstand steadfast in your faith, knowing that the same sufferings are accomplished in your brethren who are in the world. (Peter 5:8–9)

Unbelief:

> Take heed, brethren, lest haply there shall be in any one of you an evil heart of unbelief, in falling away from the living God. (Hebrews 3)

Abusing Grace:

> What shall we say then? Shall we continue in sin, that grace may abound? God forbid. We who died to sin, how shall we any longer live therein? Or are ye ignorant that all we who were baptized into Christ Jesus were baptized into his death? We were buried therefore with him through baptism into death: that like as Christ was raised from the

dead through the glory of the Father, so we also might walk in newness of life. (Romans 6:1–4)

Disobedience:

Everyone that doeth sin doeth also lawlessness; and sin is lawlessness. And ye know that he was manifested to take away sins; and in him is no sin. Whosoever abideth in him sinneth not: whosoever sinneth hath not seen him, neither knoweth him. *My* little children, let no man lead you astray: he that doeth righteousness is righteous, even as he is righteous. (1 John 3:4–7)

When we tolerate sin or refuse to forgive:

But to whom ye forgive anything, I forgive also: for what I also have forgiven, if I have forgiven anything, for your sakes have I forgiven it in the presence of Christ; that no advantage may be gained over us by Satan: for we are not ignorant of his devices. (2 Corinthians 2:10–11)

Put on your breastplate to gain the victory!

SHOES OF PEACE

For shoes, put on the peace that comes from the good news so that you will be fully prepared. In Ephesians 6, Paul tells us to stand firm with our feet fitted with the readiness that comes from the gospel of peace.

It may seem strange to consider shoes to be part of your armor, but can you imagine going to battle shoeless? You would most likely be in pain with every step, as you pass over all kinds of harsh landscape. Ultimately, it would inhibit your ability to fight.

So how can the gospel of peace be related to shoes? To start, we must understand what the gospel of peace is. The word "gospel" means "good news," referring to the sacrifice Jesus made for us so that we can be saved. As a result, this brings us peace.

As Christians, we are called to share the good news of Christ with others. Having our shoes fitted with the gospel of peace allows us to do this successfully.

John 14:27 says, "Peace I leave with you; my peace I give unto you: not as the world giveth, give I unto you. Let not your heart be troubled, neither let it be fearful." With God's strength, we can be brave in sharing our faith with others. Jesus already defeated death, so we do not need to be afraid.

Our shoes equip us to walk through rough areas. In the same way, having hope in Jesus helps us walk through the trials we face. John 16:33 says, "These things have I spoken unto you, that in me ye may have peace. In the world ye have tribulation: but be of good cheer; I have overcome the world."

Just like having a good pair of shoes can help us walk across rough terrain, having confidence in Christ allows us to boldly proclaim His name. While we may face persecution in this life, we can rest in knowing the Savior of the world loves us and cares for us. Stand firm with your feet planted, hold your ground, and get into position When Satan attacks with his flaming arrows like doubt, such as, "If God really loved you he wouldn't of let this happen," dig your peace shoes into the dirt (God's Word) and reply, "It is written: And we know that to them that love God all things work together for good, *even* to them that are called according to *his* purpose" (Romans 8:28).

In addition to standing, our ground shoes are for moving forward. Having our feet fitted with the shoes of the gospel of peace allows us to be ready to share God with others at all times. As Christians, we should always be prepared, as we never know when an opportunity may arise to share the good news of the gospel with someone else.

Be ready to stand firm no matter what the enemy brings. Ultimately, the shoes of peace equip us to fight for Christ in the spiritual battles we face.

THE SHIELD OF FAITH

In addition to all these hold up the shield of
faith to stop the fiery arrows of the devil.
—Ephesians 6:16

What is faith? Now faith is confidence in what we hope for and assurance about what we do not see. This is what the ancients were commended for. By faith, we understand that the universe was formed at God's command, so that what is seen was not made out of what was visible.

What does the shield of faith do? It stops the fiery arrows from Satan.

What are the fiery arrows from Satan, you may ask? These are Satan's attacks on us; they are those obstacles that get in our way and try to hinder our walk with God.

The writer of Hebrews wrote, "You will follow the example of those who are going to inherit God's promises because of their faith and endurance. For example, there was God's promise to Abraham…God took an oath in his own name, saying: I will certainly bless you, and I will multiply your descendants beyond number. Then Abraham waited Patiently, and he received what God had promised" (Hebrews 6:12–13). As he waited, though there were times of obstacles where he became impatient and tried to take matters into his own hands, having a son by means of a second wife. Which turned out to be a disaster, full of sorrow and pain. But there again, God came to the rescue of Abraham, and what the devil meant for bad, God made for his good. At times, he and his wife even doubted that they would even receive this promise from God at all. Sarah, the wife, even laughed in disbelief when she was told the promise was soon to come about. But in the end, Abraham received the promise, and at the end of his life, the Lord blessed him in every way.

Job also is a perfect example of faith, for Job felt that God abandoned him; he didn't realize what had taken place in the heavenly realm and that he was under attack by Satan. Even through Job's pain and hardship, he stayed faithful to God through till the end, and in turn, God blessed him with so much more in the second half of his life.

When we experience pain and loss because of something that is beyond our control, we may feel like God is our enemy. The anger and confusion we may feel don't need to destroy our faith. We may never know why God allows such trials. But at such times, we need to completely trust in God who is sovereign and will not allow us to suffer more than we can bear.

It is easy to lose faith when we are troubled. Sometimes, it seems like the storms of life are never going to end and the faith we have is slipping away. Simon Peter had his ups and downs also and he was a great apostle of God, but he too felt the storms of life. On the night Simon Peter would deny him, Jesus said to him, "Simon, Simon, behold, Satan asked to have you, that he might sift you as wheat: but I made supplication for thee, that thy faith fail not; and do thou, when once thou hast turned again, establish thy brethren" (Luke 22:31–32).

Jesus pointed out here that Simon had an enemy in the spiritual realm. Jesus knew he would be attacked and sifted, but he also was confident that afterward, Peter would return to God.

We should not be surprised that we face times when our faith seems to disappear. We may feel that we are being ripped apart. We need to dig deep at this time, hold strong to the shield of faith, and know that this, too, God will see you through.

Sometimes, what we don't realize is that our trials and tribulations throughout our lives are our lessons to make us stronger. It's like boot camp, and once we make it through, we are stronger and wiser and ready for what is to come.

Jesus warned us he said that if we followed him, we would be persecuted. In today's world, we have persecution all around us. Persecution will come, so we need to hold tight to our faith and know God will never leave or forsake us, and in the end, we will receive our glorious crown with eternal salvation!

HELMET OF SALVATION

Ephesians 6:17 instructs us to put on the whole armor of God and to "take the helmet of salvation and the sword of the Spirit, which is the word of God." When a soldier suited up for battle, the helmet was the last piece of armor to go on. It was the final act of readiness in preparation for combat. A helmet was vital for survival, protecting the brain, the command station for the rest of the body. If the head was badly damaged, the rest of the armor would be of little use.

What is the helmet of salvation?

The assurance of salvation is our impenetrable defense against anything the enemy throws at us. Jesus said, "And be not afraid of them that kill the body, but are not able to kill the soul: but rather fear him who is able to destroy both soul and body in hell" (Matthew 10:28). The idea in this verse is that, as we prepare for Satan's attacks, we must grab that helmet and buckle it tightly. Salvation is not limited to a one-time act of the past or even a future hope. God's salvation is an ongoing, eternal state that His children enjoy in the present. It is daily protection and deliverance from our sin nature and Satan's schemes.

Because of the power of the cross, our enemy no longer has any hold on us (Romans 6:10, 8:2; 1 Corinthians 1:18). He knows that, but he also knows that most of God's children do not know that—or at least, they do not live as if they know. We must learn to keep our helmets buckled so that his fiery missiles do not lodge in our thoughts and set us on fire. Through this helmet of salvation, we can destroy arguments and every lofty opinion raised against the knowledge of God and take every thought captive to obey Christ (2 Corinthians 10:5).

There are several actions a believer can take to keep this helmet fastened and functioning:

1. Renew our minds. Our minds are battlefields. The outcomes of those battles determine the course of our lives. Romans 12:1–2 instructs us to renew our minds by allowing the truth of God's Word to wipe out anything contrary to it. Old ideas, opinions, and worldviews must be replaced. We must allow God's truth to continually wash away the world's filth, lies, and confusion from our minds and adopt God's perspective.

2. Reject doubts that arise from circumstances. Human beings are sensory creatures. What we cannot fathom with our five senses, we tend to disregard. If we allow them to, circumstances may convince us that God does not really love us or that His Word is not true. It is impossible to have faith and doubt at the same time. God rewards our faith. With the helmet of salvation firmly in place, we can choose to believe what appears impossible (Hebrews 11:6; 1 Peter 1:8–9).

3. Keep an eternal perspective. When life crashes in around us, we must remember to look up. Our salvation is the most precious gift we have received. Keeping our eyes on God's promises can help us weather life's storms. We can choose to live our lives by the motto: "If it doesn't have eternal significance, it's not important" (Matthew 6:20; 1 Corinthians 3:11–13).

4. Remember that victory is already accomplished. When we consider ourselves dead to sin but alive in God (Romans 6:11), we eliminate many of the opportunities Satan uses to entrap us. When choosing sin is no longer an option for us because we recognize ourselves to be "new creatures" (2 Corinthians 5:17; 1 John 3:9), we effectively cut off many avenues of failure.

5. Find all our hope in Him. Psalm 73:25 says, "Whom have I in heaven *but thee*? And there is none upon earth that I

desire besides thee." Our helmet is most effective when we treasure what it represents. The salvation Jesus purchased for us cannot share the place of importance in our hearts with earthly things. When pleasing the Lord is our supreme delight, we eliminate many of Satan's lures and render his evil suggestions powerless.

As we wear the helmet of salvation every day, our minds become more insulated against the suggestions, desires, and traps the enemy lays for us. We choose to guard our minds from excessive worldly influence and, instead, think of things that honor Christ (Philippians 4:8). In doing so, we wear our salvation as a protective helmet that will guard our hearts and minds in Christ Jesus (Philippians 4:7; cf. Isaiah 26:3; 1 Peter 1:5).

SWORD OF THE GOSPEL

> Take the helmet of salvation and the sword of the Spirit, which is the word of God. And pray in the Spirit on all occasions with all kinds of prayers and requests. With this in mind, be alert and always keep on praying for all the Lord's people. (Ephesians 6:16–17)

The last piece of the armor that Paul talks about in Ephesians 6 is the sword of the Spirit. This is our defense, our weapon!

Paul says the sword of the Spirit is the word of God.

Looking at this, the weapon given to us to strike the enemy to fight back with is the word of God!

The purpose of the sword of the Spirit—the Bible—is to make us strong and able to withstand the evil onslaughts of Satan, our enemy (Psalm 119:11, 33–40, 99–105). The Holy Spirit uses the power of the Word to save souls and then to give them spiritual strength to be mature soldiers for the Lord in fighting this corrupt and evil world we live in. The more we know and understand the Word of God, the more useful we will be in doing the will of God and the more effective we will be in standing against the enemy of our soul. For God just didn't give us the Bible to entertain ourselves with stories at bedtime, he gave us the Bible to use as a weapon. Anytime a soldier went to battle, he made sure that his sword was ready; he did not leave it on the ground to get rusty and dull, but he gave attention to his weapon before the battle. He sharpened it and polished it; he practiced with it, so he could be ready for what awaited him. Just as a soldier does this with his sword, so should we do with God's word. We must be diligently reading and sharpening our minds. We must be practicing our moves in the ways of Jesus. We must be polishing up our scripture, so that it is written on our hearts. So that when the hard times come and it will, you are ready, and you don't fumble your sword, but your moves are precise to cut off the heads of your enemies.

Here are scriptures to sharpen our sword for battle:

> For the word of God is living, and active, and sharper than any two-edged sword, and piercing even to the dividing of soul and spirit, of both joints and marrow, and quick to discern the thoughts and intents of the heart. (Hebrews 4:12)

> Every scripture inspired of God *is* also profitable for teaching, for reproof, for correction, for instruction which is in righteousness: that the man of God may be complete, furnished completely unto every good work. (2 Timothy 3:16–17)

> For the weapons of our warfare are not of the flesh, but mighty before God to the casting down of strongholds); casting down imaginations, and every high thing that is exalted against the knowledge of God, and bringing every thought into captivity to the obedience of Christ. (2 Corinthians 10:4–5)

I have laid up your word in my heart, that I might not sin against you. (Psalms 119:11)

Teach me, O Jehovah, the way of thy statutes; And I shall keep it unto the end. Give me understanding, and I shall keep thy law; Yea, I shall observe it with my whole heart. Make me to go in the path of thy commandments; For therein do I delight. Incline my heart unto thy testimonies, and not to covetousness. Turn away mine eyes from beholding vanity, and quicken me in thy ways. Confirm unto thy servant thy word, which is in order unto the fear of thee. Turn away my reproach whereof I am afraid; For thine ordinances are good. Behold, I have longed after thy precepts: Quicken me in thy righteousness. (Psalms 119:33–40)

I have more understanding than all my teachers;
For thy testimonies are my meditation
I understand more than the aged,
Because I have kept thy precepts.
I have refrained my feet from every evil way,
That I might observe thy word.
I have not turned aside from thine ordinances;
For thou hast taught me.
How sweet are thy words unto my taste!
Yea, sweeter than honey to my mouth!
Through thy precepts I get understanding:
Therefore I hate every false way. (Psalms 119:99–105)

GOD IS CLOSE TO THOSE WHO ARE SUFFERING

What is constant throughout Scripture is that God provides comfort to the suffering and meets the needs of the brokenhearted (Psa. 34:18; Psa. 145:18). His Word promises that those who are in the midst of suffering, whether experiencing death or depression, have the hope that everything is working together for the good of those who love him and are called according to his purpose (Rom. 8:28). It is outside of God's character to senselessly torment those he loves (Lam. 3:31–33). We know that the trials that we are experiencing on this earth, while difficult and uncomfortable, are for the testing of our faith (James 1:2), to produce endurance and character (Rom. 5:3–5) and are never without purpose.

THE VICTORY!

No victory is ever easy to come by if it has meaning. Some victories are lesser than others, but the biggest victories come with the greatest rewards.

Jesus said the road to hell is wide and easy and many will take it, but the road to everlasting life is narrow and hard and only a few will take this road.

When we are truly ready for God to take over our lives, we must truly be ready to give up all sin. This road will be hard because there will be no substitutes. For many of us that come off addiction, we don't want to go through the hard part (sickness); for many, that's what holds them back from becoming clean, but it is that hard road that leads to the victory. We cannot jump from one drug to another. It is like trading the black monkey on your back for a red one. Through my many years of addiction, I tried this method. I thought that the answer was in weed. "It's natural," I would tell myself. But then again, I could say that for most drugs. Opium, cocaine, peyote—hmmm, all come from plants.

Do you see how we make excuses for drugs so that we can continue using them?

I have many friends I've seen fall to this deception. They get off the "hard stuff" and think another drug or addiction is the answer. After a while though, they are back in the same boat, but this time, their boat is sinking even faster. They have multiple demons now as the scripture says in Matthew 12:43–45, "When an impure spirit comes out of a person, it goes through arid places seeking rest and does not find it. Then it says, 'I will return to the house I left.' When it arrives, it finds the house unoccupied, swept clean and put in order. Then it goes and takes with it seven other spirits more wicked than itself, and they go in and live there. And the final condition of that person is worse than the first." We have to understand that God did not create our bodies to be dependent on a drug. In fact, quite the opposite: our bodies were made in perfection. God wants us to be dependent on him.

Paul speaks in acts to the Greeks and Jews about the good news of who Jesus is and why he came. Paul also performed many miracles in the name of Jesus. God blessed Paul and gave him authority to cast out demons through the Name of Jesus. News spread fast of this Jesus that Paul preached about and his name became honored and feared throughout the region.

> When this became known to the Jews and Greeks living in Ephesus, they were all seized with fear, and the name of the Lord Jesus was held in high honor. Many of those who believed now came and openly confessed what they had done. A number who had practiced sorcery brought their scrolls together and burned them publicly. When they calculated the value of the scrolls, the total came to fifty thousand drachmas. In this way the word of the Lord spread widely and grew in power. (Acts 19:17–22)

Do you see the connection here? These people were sinners who practiced sorcery (pharmacia) and idol worship. They were sinners living in darkness engulfed in the world of sin. When they heard the good news of Jesus and how he could heal them they believed. They even burned their books; you have to understand these were not just any books, they were very expensive books (worth millions) that had been in their families for generations. When the people of Ephesus decided to turn their lives over to Jesus, they had no problem chucking them in the fire in the square. The fear and love they held for Jesus outweighed their tradition and their prestige. They were willing to give up everything, and they did. Could you? They would be mocked from now on by others in the town and great persecution from the government. I'm sure a lot of them went to prison for their belief in Jesus. Are you willing to give up your life? Because, my friend, when we turn our lives over to God, our reward is eternal life with him which is beyond any priceless gift we could get on this earth.

WHAT WE GET WHEN WE BELIEVE IN JESUS

When we believe in Jesus, we receive healing.

> And as Jesus passed by from thence, two blind men followed him, crying out, and saying, "Have mercy on us, thou son of David." And when he was come into the house, the blind men came to him: and Jesus saith unto them, "Believe ye that I am able to do this?" They say unto him, "Yea, Lord." Then touched he their eyes, saying, "According to your faith be it done unto you." (Matthew 9:27–29)

When we believe Jesus, he answers prayers.

> And Jesus answering saith unto them, "Have faith in God. Verily I say unto you, Whosoever shall say unto this mountain, Be thou taken up and cast into the sea; and shall not doubt in his heart, but shall believe that what he saith cometh to pass; he shall have it. Therefore I say unto you,

All things whatsoever ye pray and ask for, believe that ye receive them, and ye shall have them." (Mark 11:22–24)

When we believe in Jesus and begin to follow him, we receive a new life with a new identity.

Therefore, if anyone is in Christ, he is a new creation; old things have passed away; behold, all things have become new. (2 Corinthians 5:17)

OUR MISSION

A life set free from all addiction by the Lord is a beautiful sight to behold. When we share our experiences and obey the word of God, people will see the glory of God in our lives and gain hope. We know from experience the depths of suffering pain and brokenness. We know the pain of being enslaved to our passions and blinded to our denial. We have endured our time of grieving. We can relate to those who struggle to be free. We also now know there is more to life than bondage. In Jesus, there is healing and freedom, truth and mercy, beauty and joy. When Jesus came to the earth, he had a mission, which was to bring the good news to the poor, to comfort the broken-hearted to proclaim that captives will be set free. Isaiah 61:3 tells us that he will give a crown of beauty for ashes and joyous blessing instead of mourning, festive praise instead of despair. This mission that Jesus was on has been passed on to us. Some people talk about preaching the gospel, but then alienate those who need the good news the most. We are in a unique position to share our experiences, our strengths, and our hope in a way that broken people can understand and receive it.

May this book help you find your way to God. May God bless you and give you strength. I pray that my testimony may be an inspiration of God's goodness in your life and that God will use you in mighty ways to bring his message to others.

All glory be to the Father, the Son, and the Holy Spirit, Amen. Thank you for reading.

RESOURCES AND REFERENCES

https://erlc.com/resource-library/articles/what-does-the-bible-say-about-mental-illness/

https://www.gcu.edu/blog/spiritual-life/weekly-devotional-armor-god-shoes-gospel-peace

https://bible.knowing-jesus.com/Hebrews/3/12

https://www.gotquestions.org/helmet-of-salvation.html

https://bible.knowing-jesus.com/topics/Relationship-Of-Men-And-Women

http://www.freebiblestudyguides.org/bible-teachings/armor-of-god-breasplate-of-righteousness.htm

https://www.gospeltractandbible.org/tract/forgiveness?gclid=EAIaI-QobChMIrvCdkLWm8gIVwhmtBh3XdA0TEAAYAyAAE-gKHcvD_BwE

https://www.thetimesherald.com/story/life/faith/2017/02/03/hayes-choose-stand-god-world/97437366/

https://info.gonow.org/go-evangelism-what-the-bible-says-about-fear/?gclid=Cj0KCQjw5JSLBhCxARIsAHgO2SdditGRzjjFI-JpmXWGOXlTnokWF8GFd0O5WxwrnXhQzD2Y7ZrHxS-RwaAoBpEALw_wcB

https://www.lifeway.com/en/articles/pastor-depression-eight-bibli-cal-strategies-for-counseling-depression

www.Lifeway.com

https://jesus.net/the_life_of_jesus/the-bio-of-a-word/?gclid=C-j0KCQiAnaeNBhCUARIsABEee8VwVlGuMfae1lOeWqPr-2r9kIZDD5ETUJ05ane8VHsG8iLQCJu3BpPEaAp-pQEALw_wcB

https://www.biblegateway.com/passage/?search=2%20Corinthians
%205%3A17-18&version=NIV
https://saddlebackleather.com/signs-of-pride
Pharmacia: The Biblical View of Drug Use by Robert A. Orem Jr.
Life Recovery 12-Step Bible

ABOUT THE AUTHOR

My time in prison allowed me to walk with God 24–7. I learned many lessons and also saw many great and mighty things the Lord was doing. While in prison, I enrolled in a biblical study program and received my ordination. I began preaching while in prison. I fell in love with telling others about Jesus and his love for us. Today, I live in a small town in New Mexico called Espanola. It is a beautiful valley, where just like everywhere else, people are struggling with addiction. I continued preaching when I was released in all the local churches and local Christian TV stations that would allow me to testify. I now hold weekly Bible study classes called Breaking the Chains through the Life Recovery Bible that encircles addiction that plagues us all. I also manage a homeless shelter, which is the first in our town; it is such a humbling experience. The people I meet are such amazing good-hearted people that have just gotten lost or have fallen to hard times along the way. Working at the shelter allows me to talk with those struggling with addiction about the Lord and how there is a way out. I am so grateful to Father God every day for what he has done in my life and how having a relationship with Jesus has changed my life.

Lightning Source UK Ltd.
Milton Keynes UK
UKHW011011171222
414082UK00001B/134

9 798885 405287